Joan of Arc

Joan of Arc, from a painting by Albert Lynch. © Bettman/CORBIS

JOAN OF ARC

The Warrior Saint

Stephen W. Richey

Westport, Connecticut
London

Library of Congress Cataloging-in-Publication Data

Richey, Stephen W., 1957–
 Joan of Arc : the warrior saint / by Stephen W. Richey
  p. cm.
 Includes bibliographical references and index.
 ISBN 0–275–98103–7 (alk. paper)
 1. Joan, of Arc, Saint, 1412–1431. 2. Joan, of Arc, Saint, 1412–1431—Military leadership. 3. Christian saints—France—Biography. 4. France—History—Charles VII, 1422–1461. I. Title.
DC103.R52   2003
944′.026′092—dc21   2003045763
[B]

British Library Cataloguing in Publication Data is available.

Copyright © 2003 by Stephen W. Richey

All rights reserved. No portion of this book may be
reproduced, by any process or technique, without the
express written consent of the publisher.

Library of Congress Catalog Car Number: 2003045763
ISBN: 0–275–98103–7

First published in 2003

Praeger Publishers, 88 Post Road West, Westport, CT 06881
An imprint of Greenwood Publishing Group, Inc.
www.praeger.com

Printed in the United States of America

The paper used in this book complies with the
Permanent Paper Standard issued by the National
Information Standards Organization (Z39.48–1984).

10 9 8 7 6 5 4 3 2 1

*Pour Jehanne La Pucelle,
que j'aime de tout mon coeur.*

CONTENTS

Illustrations   ix

1. The Two Key Questions about Joan of Arc's Military Career: "What" and "How"   1
2. The Story of Joan's Story: A Review of the Literature   7
3. The General Situation Prior to Joan's Arrival on the Public Stage   13
4. Joan's Military Career: The Preliminaries   25
5. Joan's Achievement in Raising French Morale: The First Part of "What"   37
6. Joan's Achievement as a Military Commander: The Second Part of "What"   45
7. Joan's Leadership Qualities: The First Part of "How"   89
8. Joan's Lucky Circumstances: The Second Part of "How"   115
9. Summation   121

Appendix A: Joan's Four Key Missions or Prophecies   123
Appendix B: Joan of Arc at the Movies   125

Appendix C: Joan's Personal Appearance	139
Notes	143
Selected Bibliography	167
Index	171

ILLUSTRATIONS

PHOTOGRAPHS

1.1	World War I poster invokes Joan as it urges American women to support the war effort	2
4.1	German tapestry depicts Joan arriving at the castle of Chinon for her first meeting with the Dauphin Charles	31
4.2	Painting of the Dauphin Charles by Jean Fouquet	33
6.1	Joan's entry into the streets of Orléans, as depicted by the nineteenth-centrury painter, J. J. Scherrer	53
6.2	The home of Jacques Boucher, treasurer of the city of Orléans, where Joan stayed during her time in the city	54
6.3	Joan leads the attack on the Tourelles	62
6.4	Statue of Joan in the great cathedral at Reims	78
6.5	Official document awarding titles of nobility to Joan and her family	82
7.1	Equestrian statue of Joan in Paris	107
C.1	"Doodle" of Joan in the margin of an official document of the Burgundian government of Paris	140

MAPS

1.1	France 1429	3
3.1	Agincourt: October 25, 1415	18
4.1	Northern France	27
6.1	The Siege of Orléans: October 12, 1428 to April 29, 1429	48
6.2	Joan Breaks the Siege: May 4–8, 1429	58
6.3	The Loire River Campaign: June 12–18, 1429	68
6.4	The Coronation Journey: June 30–July 17, 1429	76

Chapter 1

THE TWO KEY QUESTIONS ABOUT JOAN OF ARC'S MILITARY CAREER: "WHAT" AND "HOW"

She was a teenage farm girl who crowned a reluctant king, rallied a broken people, reversed the course of a great war, and pushed history onto a new path. She was Joan of Arc—what are we to make of her? The people who came after her in the five centuries since her death tried to make everything of her: demonic fanatic, spiritual mystic, naive and tragically ill-used tool of the powerful, creator and icon of modern popular nationalism, adored heroine, saint. She insisted, even when threatened with torture and faced with death by fire, that she was guided by voices from God. Voices or no voices, her achievements leave those who know her story shaking their heads in amazed wonder.[1] The military historian in particular may find himself transfixed by the image of the girl in armor who put new life into a moribund army and who led that army to victory. As a military historian, he will feel a need first to understand exactly *what* Joan did as a soldier, and second, to explain *how* she did what she did.

Joan was born into a common family of the peasant village of Domrémy in the French province of Lorraine in about 1412. She grew up as an unusually devout farm child during the height of the Hundred Years' War. Disaster after disaster befell her native France. The English invaders and their Burgundian allies conquered and occupied the northern half of France, including Paris. The English also maintained their hold on a large enclave in the southwest of France. The Dauphin Charles, the uncrowned king of France, set up the remnants of his royal court at the town of Chinon. From here, this weak monarch tried to rule over the unoccupied rem-

Photo 1.1 Joan of Arc has been used—and abused—as an icon for any number of political and social causes over the centuries. This World War I poster invokes Joan as it urges American women to support the war effort. © Library of Congress.

nant of France. Starting in May 1428, Joan—claiming that God was directing her through voices she heard—repeatedly approached the commander of the nearest military garrison loyal to Charles. She demanded that he send her to Charles at Chinon. She insisted that it was her divinely ordered mission to lead the French army to victory over the English and escort Charles to Reims, where he would be properly crowned king. In October 1428, the English, later joined by the Burgundians, began their siege of the city of Orléans, their last obstacle before overrunning the rest

Map 1.1 France 1429

of France. In February 1429, the local garrison commander finally relented and sent Joan to Chinon with a small escort. Upon arriving at Chinon, she presented herself to Charles with her hair cut short and wearing a man's clothes, though she made it clear to all that she was in fact a girl. By April, she persuaded Charles to provide her with a horse, a suit of armor, a sword, and a banner, and to place her at the head of the army marching to rescue Orléans. Upon arriving at Orléans, she proceeded to lead the army in an astounding series of victories that reversed the tide of the war. She was about seventeen years old. In July 1429, she led both the army and the timid Charles deep into enemy-occupied territory to the great cathedral at Reims, where France's kings had been crowned for generations. With Joan in armor at his side, Charles received the crown.

After thus becoming fully king, Charles sought to undercut Joan's influence in any way he could. To Joan's rage, he opened negotiations with the Burgundians and disbanded the army while much of France was still under hostile occupation. Joan continued to make war on her own, leading such meager forces as she was allowed. It was in this capacity that she was taken prisoner by enemy soldiers at the siege of Compiègne in May 1430. A church court of English-sponsored clerics convicted her of heresy and she died at the stake in May 1431, at about the age of nineteen. Charles resumed military operations and succeeded in driving the English from France by 1453, thus winning the Hundred Years' War. In 1456, the Church revoked Joan's conviction for heresy and proclaimed that she had been a good Christian and Catholic. The Church canonized her as a saint in 1920.[2]

Whatever politicians, pundits, and ordinary people since Joan's time have tried to make of her as an icon for this or that cause, one thing remains unassailably true. Her impact on history derives from her success in the realm of *action*. Everything in her legacy flows from her mounting the stage of history in a shining suit of armor, astride a great war horse, brandishing her banner and shouting, "Follow me!" to an army of soldiers who adored her. She was a military leader. But what kind of military leader was she? Was she nothing more than a charismatic, but naive, inspirational mascot who was cynically used by the real military leaders to rally their demoralized troops? Or was she a true commander who made decisions and gave orders? Respectfully setting aside voices from God for the moment, how did an illiterate peasant girl with no military training lead an army that had known nothing but humiliation and defeat to sudden, repeated, and decisive victories?

Before attempting to answer *how* Joan did what she did as a military leader, it is first necessary to reach a conclusion as to *what* she did. Modern scholars disagree on the "what" before they even get to the "how." Frenchman Edouard Perroy, in his book *The Hundred Years War,* implies that Joan was nothing but an inspirational figurehead, a sort of all-army "cheerleader." Perroy claims that Joan "knew nothing about the art of war, and thought that abstaining from oaths and brothels was enough to earn victory for the soldiers." Perroy goes on to assert that Joan "did not lead" the troops, leaving that duty to the established captains of the army. He writes, "She was content to exhort the combatants, say what advice her voices gave, step into the breach at critical moments and rally the infantry."[3] American author Frances Gies, in her book *Joan of Arc: The Legend and the Reality,* specifically cites Perroy in order to take issue with him. She maintains that Joan was a true war captain who listened and spoke in war councils, who advocated courses of action, and who made decisions and gave orders.[4] Over the last century, career officers of the French army have done much of the writing on Joan's career as a soldier. These authors are unanimous in depicting Joan as a genuine military genius who was absolutely in charge of fighting her part of the Hundred Years' War. Colonel Ferdinand de Liocourt extols Joan's martial qualities in his two-volume work, *La mission de Jeanne d'Arc.* He writes, "The Maid acted following the equilibrium of faculties that Napoleon considered fundamental for assuring a great command." De Liocourt explains elsewhere in his work what he means by the "equilibrium of faculties." This equilibrium is the necessary balance between a commander's refinement of intellect that enables him (her!) to plan a battle and his/her toughness of character that enables him/her to *fight* a battle. De Liocourt maintains that Joan possessed this balance in superlative measure, as when he writes, "She thus showed herself bold in conception, methodical in preparation, prompt in decision, ardent in execution, obstinate in the presence of the enemy's reactions."[5] In his book *Jeanne d'Arc, Chef de Guerre: Le génie militaire et politique de Jeanne d'Arc, Campagne de France 1429–1430,* Lieutenant-Colonel de Lancesseur is even more extravagant than de Liocourt in his praise of Joan's gift for war. He states in his conclusion that "the military genius of Joan of Arc is a great proof of the existence of God."[6]

There is an extreme divergence in views between Perroy on one side and Gies, de Liocourt, and, especially, de Lancesseur on the other regarding what Joan really did as a soldier. Given the stature of these authors, it seems a daunting task to find the truth of what Joan did as a military leader. Nonetheless, the question of what she did must be resolved. Only then can a historian address the subsequent question of how Joan did what she did on the battlefields of the Hundred Years' War.

The purpose of this book is to describe what Joan did as a soldier and then to attempt to explain how she did it. This book will *not* follow a strictly chronological pattern. First, it will be necessary to review the literature that has been written about Joan, a body of literature that started to grow when she was still alive and that continues to grow in the present day. Next, it will be useful to describe at length the social, political, and military situation of Joan's world as it existed when she began her short but intense career. Next will come a chapter briefly narrating the course of Joan's life from her birth to the day she first placed herself at the head of the French army. Then it will be time to get to the substance of this book. Two chapters will describe the "what" of Joan's military career. The first of these two chapters will focus on Joan's role in raising French morale, and the second will focus on her role as a strategist and battlefield commander who made decisions and gave orders that her soldiers obeyed. Finally, two chapters will attempt to analyze the "how" of Joan's martial achievements. Both these chapters will necessarily be more speculative than anything that has gone before. The first of these chapters will assess Joan's qualities of intellect and character that enabled her to lead her soldiers so well. The second will enumerate the lucky circumstances that Joan was able to exploit so successfully as she fulfilled her mission for France.

Chapter 2

THE STORY OF JOAN'S STORY: A REVIEW OF THE LITERATURE

Any attempt to find where the truth about Joan's military skill lies must of course return to the firsthand sources. In the case of Joan of Arc, scholars are richly blessed by the great volume and detail of the accounts of Joan by those who knew her personally—accounts that have been kept scrupulously intact to this day. Most of what we know about Joan comes from the transcripts of her two trials. In 1431, Joan, at that time a prisoner of war of her English enemies, was subjected to a Church trial for heresy. The trial was a political sham, conducted by turncoat French clerics who were partisans of the English and who were dependent on English support to maintain their privileged positions. To no one's surprise, they found Joan guilty and condemned her to death at the stake. The complete original transcript of her trial, including her own account of her life, still exists, in good condition, at French archives in our own time. In 1455, twenty-four years after Joan's death, the Church reopened her case by giving her a posthumous retrial. In various inquiries preceding and during the retrial, 115 witnesses who had known Joan answered questions about her.[1] The court recorded their testimonies in hundreds of pages of writing that are fully intact today. The witnesses included people from all backgrounds, including peasants who were childhood friends of Joan, lords and ladies who had known her at the royal court, and, most importantly for the present purpose, soldiers who had gone into battle at Joan's side. The retrial, besides nullifying Joan's conviction for heresy and opening the way for her eventual canonization, provided scholars of subsequent generations with more firsthand source material about Joan than exists for almost any other historical figure who lived prior to her time. Perhaps less reliable than the transcripts of the retrial, but still valuable, are the various chronicles that were penned during or shortly after Joan's lifetime and that are still in existence in various archives.

Modern published works on Joan of Arc number in the thousands, but the foundation of all serious scholarship about her is formed by the transcripts of her trial and retrial, together with the chronicles written within a few years of her death. Modern scholarship about Joan began in the years 1841–1849. During those years, the Frenchman Jules Quicherat completed one of the most tremendous feats of scholarship and editorship of all time. He collected, edited, and published in five volumes the transcripts of Joan's trial and retrial, the letters she herself dictated to scribes, numerous letters written about Joan by her contemporaries, and all the chronicles written about Joan during or shortly after her time on this earth. Joan's trial fills Quicherat's first volume and her retrial his second and part of his third. Both trial transcripts are in Latin in Quicherat's opus. The various chronicles fill Quicherat's fourth volume. The most valuable of the chronicles are those written by Perceval de Cagny and Jean Chartier and the anonymously authored chronicles known as the *Journal of the Siege of Orléans* and the *Chronicle of the Maid*. Quicherat presents these chronicles in their archaic but still readable French. His fifth volume is filled with poetry and dozens of letters, both those dictated by Joan and those written about her by others. Some of these pieces are in Latin and others in French. Also in volume five are excerpts from official financial ledger books of Joan's day showing, for example, how much public money was spent to buy her suit of armor and how much to lodge her father at the Striped Donkey Inn in Reims for Charles's coronation.[2]

Even after the passage of over a century and a half, Quicherat's work has been only partly superseded by more recent scholars. Pierre Tisset and Yvonne Lanhers edited and published Joan's trial transcript during the period 1960–1971[3] while Pierre Duparc edited and published the now definitive version of her retrial transcript from 1977 to 1989.[4] Thanks to these works, most of the transcripts of both trials are now easily available in French. However, Quicherat's volumes remain the only source where one can easily find the various chronicles and letters.

Secondary works about Joan range from serious scholarship to less well supported medical theories about the "real" source of her "voices" and various conspiracy theories claiming that the "real" Joan escaped death at the stake. An indispensable aid in judging the merits of secondary works about

Joan is the book *Joan of Arc in History, Literature, and Film* by Sorbonne graduate Nadia Margolis, published in 1990. Her book is an immense annotated bibliography listing and assessing 1,516 primary-source documents, secondary-source books and journal articles, and movies about Joan.[5] Margolis's judgments of the relative value of various works about Joan provide a valuable foundation for research on the Maid of Orléans.

The first serious scholarly secondary works about Joan were written by Quicherat's contemporary, Frenchman Jules Michelet. Michelet was an ardent patriot, and today his works on Joan read more like secular hagiography than anything else. Michelet was more responsible than anyone for causing Joan to "take off" as the passionately embraced symbol of French nationalism. Still, Michelet shares the credit with Quicherat for first making Joan a standard topic of modern scholarship. Margolis describes Michelet's work as the "[p]ivotal, most influential work on J' for [the] modern era."[6]

The first notable American work about Joan was the novelized biography titled *Personal Recollections of Joan of Arc*, written by none other than Mark Twain. The man who was already famous for *Tom Sawyer* and *Huckleberry Finn* adored Joan and unabashedly claimed his book about her to be his best and favorite piece of work. Margolis notes Twain's "warmth" for his subject and the fact that Twain became well versed in Quicherat and Michelet while doing his research for his novelization of Joan's life.[7]

In 1908, Frenchman Anatole France, a witty iconoclast who loathed the Church, published his biography of Joan that belittled her accomplishments. He depicted her as the brave but naive pawn of the powerful people around her. Margolis describes France's book as the "most famous and provocative of typologically negative J' biogs.," but she also states that France's view of Joan "goes against historical evidence."[8]

Within a year of France publishing his book, Scotsman Andrew Lang, making thorough use of Quicherat, published a biography that rebutted France. Lang argued that Joan was a true genius who knew exactly what she was doing as she played a pivotal role in reversing the course of the Hundred Years' War. Margolis opines of Lang's book that it is "a bit romantic for modern tastes" but "still worthwhile, solidly researched—more reliable than France's."[9]

Between the World Wars, V. Sackville-West produced her biography of Joan that remains the standard work in the English language to this day. Like Lang, Sackville-West saw Joan as the brilliant master of her own career. Sackville-West's book is a popular rather than scholarly piece of work, but it has yet to be surpassed in the English language for its completeness and depth of detail. Margolis declares that Sackville-West's work is "considered [the] best English-lang. biog. of J': balanced, well-researched, carefully presented."[10] Although Sackville-West's book is a popular biography, it is still an invaluable tool for a scholar of Joan.

Another useful English-language biography of Joan is *Joan of Arc: The Legend and the Reality* by Frances Gies. Margolis praises Gies's book as "clearly-presented, comprehensive, well-documented without being cumbersome."[11] A strong point of Gies's book that is relevant to the question under discussion is her argument that Joan was a military commander in the full sense of the term.

Edward A. Lucie-Smith's *Joan of Arc* provides a solidly comprehensive narrative of Joan's life, but his occasional forays into speculation regarding Joan's inner psychological state may grate on some readers. Despite this, Margolis characterizes Lucie-Smith's psychological biography as "one of the better attempts in this direction, most readable."[12]

After World War II, Frenchwoman Régine Pernoud became the doyenne of Joan scholarship. Her *Joan of Arc by Herself and Her Witnesses* and *The Retrial of Joan of Arc* both contain massive excerpts from all the documents first collected by Quicherat. Pernoud interweaves en bloc quotations from the original documents with her own lucid commentary and analysis. Pernoud aligned with Lang and Sackville-West in portraying Joan as a great woman (girl) of history who drove events forward by her own high intelligence and courage. When Pernoud's great works were translated into English, English speakers obtained their best-ever access to Joan's story. Margolis states that Pernoud's *Joan of Arc by Herself and Her Witnesses* is "often considered the best French biog. of J' by the best-known and most prolific living authority." Margolis praises Pernoud's "elegantly rendered commentary" in *The Retrial of Joan of Arc*.[13]

An important recent work about Joan that defies categorization is *Joan of Arc: The Image of Female Heroism* by Marina Warner. The first chapters of Warner's book are a straightforward biography of Joan, but the subsequent chapters offer provocative analyses of the many different iconic roles that Joan has played, both during her life and over the centuries since her death. Margolis praises Warner's book as a "lively, insightful, multi-dimensional cultural history of J."[14]

In recent years, scholarship about Joan has become more specialized. Two important books that came out too recently to be reviewed by Margolis are *The Interrogation of Joan of Arc,* by Karen Sullivan, and *Joan of*

Arc: The Early Debate, by Deborah A. Fraioli. Sullivan detailed dissection of the wording of the transcripts of Joan heresy that seeks to put those words in their "historical, so gious context" (as the blurb on the back cover claims). Fraio.. deeply probing analysis of the writings of various learned contemporaries of Joan who were trying to explain her significance to the educated classes of Europe.[15]

In recent decades, much of the French-language scholarship about Joan's military career has been done by officers of the French army. Two notable books in this genre —by Colonel Ferdinand de Liocourt and by Lieutenant-Colonel de Lancesseur—were cited above. Michel de Lombarès's journal article on Joan's victory at the Battle of Patay is also useful. Margolis describes de Liocourt's huge, two-volume opus as an "impressive work," but she merely notes that de Lancesseur is "another military expert praising J' as [a] military leader." She lists de Lombarès's article but offers no assessment of it.[16] The outstanding French-language scholar of recent years on the topic of medieval warfare is Professor Philippe Contamine of the Universities of Nancy and Paris. His major book on the subject has been translated into English as *War in the Middle Ages*. Also noteworthy are his journal articles "Les armées française et anglaise a l'époque de Jeanne d'Arc" and "La guerre de siège au temps de Jeanne d'Arc."[17] Both make only passing mention of Joan despite her name being in their titles. These articles are actually minutely technical treatises on various aspects of the art of war as it was practiced in Joan's time. Margolis does not list these three works by Contamine.

English-language scholarship specifically addressing Joan's role as a soldier who commanded other soldiers seems to be limited to the work you are now reading and to three recent works by Dr. Kelly DeVries of Loyola College in Baltimore. DeVries's works came out too recently to be included in Margolis's grand annotated bibliography. His essay "The Use of Gunpowder Weaponry by and against Joan of Arc during the Hundred Years War" appeared in 1996. I cited DeVries's essay "A Woman as Leader of Men" above. DeVries's recent book, *Joan of Arc: A Military Leader*, does an excellent job relating the "what" of Joan's military career. DeVries argues convincingly that Joan was, as the title of his book implies, a true military leader who had direct impact on the conduct of the war. However, DeVries does not venture a detailed analysis that attempts to explain the underlying "how" of Joan's career as a soldier. Any analysis that addresses the "how" of Joan's career must inevitably be far more speculative than an analysis that addresses only the "what." DeVries chose not to risk such speculation when he wrote his book, admirably solid as his book is.[18]

In sum, Joan of Arc is the subject of a staggering quantity of scholarship that addresses numerous specialized topics beyond merely retelling her life story. However, until now, the only serious English-language scholarship focusing directly on Joan's military career has been found in the highly praiseworthy works of Kelly DeVries. All scholars of Joan are in his debt. The book you hold in your hands will build on the solid foundation established by DeVries. This book will recapitulate the well-established "what" of Joan's military career and then contribute something new by embarking on the much more risky quest of explaining the "how" of her amazing martial achievements.

Chapter 3

THE GENERAL SITUATION PRIOR TO JOAN'S ARRIVAL ON THE PUBLIC STAGE

The Hundred Years' War formed the context of Joan's career, and the late Middle Ages, in turn, formed the context of the Hundred Years' War. A factor of late medieval culture that had a crucial impact on Joan's character, and on how both friends and enemies regarded her, was the intense religiosity of the time. For people of all social classes in Joan's time and place, intense religious faith was an omnipresent force in life. People of all levels of education saw in events both great and small the direct action of God and His saints and angels—or, conversely, the direct action of the Devil and his demons. Bad luck in a business transaction, a bountiful harvest, or victory or defeat in a great battle were all the direct result of divine or diabolical intervention.[1]

During this period of intense popular religious faith, charismatic individuals who claimed to be recipients of divine revelations were quite common. People of this sort tended to attract public followings and to command the attention of the high born and the powerful. When Joan publicly proclaimed that she was taking orders from God to crown the Dauphin Charles king and lead his army to victory, the mentality of the time led people of all levels of education to take her seriously. The question in peoples' minds was not so much whether she was inspired by God or delusional, but whether she was inspired by God or by the Devil. As the peasant-girl army commander began to win victory after victory, her French followers naturally, and sincerely, acclaimed her to be inspired by God. Her English and Burgundian enemies naturally, and sincerely, denounced her as being in league with the Devil. The religion-based loyalty of Joan's followers was her great strength and the religion-based hatred of her enemies was the cause of her hideous death.[2]

A second factor that had a profound impact on Joan was that by the early fifteenth century, most peasants in Western Europe had shaken off the restrictions of serfdom and were able to exercise some autonomy in shaping their own destinies, even if they still comprised the bottom row of building blocks in the social pyramid. Joan grew up in a village in which her family and her neighbors, despite their low birth, were well practiced in taking collective action on their own initiative to provide at least some protection for themselves and their property against the rapaciousness of freebooting local warlords. This growing sense of their own strength among the peasantry of Joan's day probably encouraged her to see herself as something more than a hopelessly downtrodden victim who could do nothing to affect her own fate and the fates of her family and neighbors. By extension, she may have been encouraged by the autonomous solidarity of her peasant community to embark on her career.[3]

A third key factor influencing Joan's career was a direct result of the Hundred Years' War itself. Under the protracted strains of the war—a war in which the English had to ship their armies across the English Channel to get them to the battlefield—the organizational structure of armies changed drastically.[4] Previously in the Middle Ages, most armies on Western European battlefields had largely been formed on the basis of vassals fulfilling feudal obligations of service to their lords. According to the social strictures of feudalism, every vassal was subject to being called up for forty days per year of obligatory military service to his lord. A great duke owed forty days' military service to his king per year, a middling-powerful noble owed forty days to his duke, a knight owed forty days to the middling-powerful noble to whom he had sworn fealty, and the peasants on the knight's manor owed the knight forty days. Whenever a vassal of any level reported to his lord for duty, that vassal brought *his* vassals along with him. For a nobleman of whatever rank who was trying to conduct a war, the great advantage of this system was that his underlings *owed* him forty days of military service per year as a social obligation. Those performing their yearly forty days of military duty expected no pay and received none. The obvious disadvantage to this system was that a military leader at any level had forty days in any given year in which to win his war, at the end of which time, his army would evaporate.

Even before the start of the Hundred Years' War, leaders of Western European armies made use of paid mercenaries in an effort to give some stability to their armies. The protracted stresses of the Hundred Years' War made the old-style feudal method of raising an army more and more unworkable. For the English especially, who had to get their troops across the Channel before they could even cross swords with the enemy, the forty-day restriction of traditional feudal obligatory service was an absurdity. English monarchs came to rely on the practice of letting out contracts among their subjects to raise formed groups of soldiers, of all social classes, who would serve overseas for the entire duration of a military campaign in return for monetary pay. The English soldiers who served in France under these conditions were not "mercenaries" in the pejorative sense of that word. They felt genuine personal loyalty to the monarchs and great nobles who led them and there was no danger they might change sides if the French offered them higher pay. Still, the English soldiers who sailed to France in the pay of their king could not yet be described as comprising either a "professional" or a "standing" army. They did, however, represent a significant first step toward the creation of true professional standing armies.

The high effectiveness of English armies of this period was partly an outgrowth of the unique social structure of England. Unlike the other feudal states on the Continent, England possessed a large, prosperous, rural, free-commoner class: the yeomen. The nobles of England not only trusted these free English commoners with highly effective weapons of war, such as the longbow; they gladly recruited these longbow-armed free commoners into their armies. On the Continent, by contrast, no member of the noble class trusted the local rural peasants enough to permit them to have weapons of such effectiveness as the longbow.

The French likewise had to move away from the traditional feudal method of raising armies; but, until the very last years of the war, French attempts at military reform were slow, halting, and only partially effective compared to the reforms of the English. Still, by the time of Joan's arrival on the scene, it is significant that one of the Dauphin Charles's major problems was a lack of money with which to *pay* Frenchmen who were loyal to fight for him. This fact signals that, by this stage of the war, the French had largely moved beyond the traditional system of feudal obligation to raise their armies. Indeed, as will be seen, one of Joan's great achievements was to use the power of her charisma to persuade Frenchmen of all social classes to serve the higher cause of France with little or no pay.[5]

Just as the French lagged behind the English in military organization, so too did they lag behind the English in developing practical attitudes about the conduct of war. Until the final phase of the Hundred Years' War, many

French knights continued to see war as an arena in which to display their chivalrous qualities, not as an instrument of state policy. In a sense, they were more concerned with showing chivalrous good form on the battlefield than they were with winning. In their own minds, they put more emphasis on valorous deeds performed in a "fair" fight against their opposing social peers than they did on subtleties of strategy or tactics that could provide an "unfair" advantage. From the beginning of the Hundred Years' War, the English had the much more modern, "professional" attitude that war was about efficient mass killing in order to achieve a political objective.[6]

During the late Middle Ages, the foremost book of advice and guidance for French knights was *The Book of Chivalry,* written by the foremost French knight of the age, Geoffroi de Charny.[7] De Charny provided his noble readers with many pages that urged upon them the chivalrous warrior virtues of courage, strength, honorable behavior, and so forth. By contrast, de Charny's treatment of the technical aspects of war fighting was brief in length and general in nature.[8] De Charny's own military career epitomized the values of honor and courage, but his record of material success on the battlefields of the Hundred Years' War was spotty. He won rightful renown for his part in the victorious defense of the towns of Tournai and Béthune against attacks by the English and Flemish in the years 1340 and 1346 respectively. However, at the Battle of Morlaix in 1342, he bravely led a horse-mounted frontal charge that met disastrous defeat at the hands of well-disciplined and cleverly positioned English troops. His death in battle at the catastrophic French defeat at Poitiers in 1356 was heroic, glorious, and futile.[9] De Charny's writings, life, and death embodied all that was noble and all that was self-defeating in the French conduct of war.

The desperate situation of France that drove Joan to undertake her quest was a long time in the making. The century-long struggle between the intricately intermarried noble houses of England and France for control of the French throne began in 1337.[10] The opening years of the Hundred Years' War saw crushing English victories over the French at Sluys in 1340, Morlaix in 1342, Auberoche in 1345, Crécy in 1346, Mauron in 1352, and Poitiers in 1356. At the entrance of Sluys harbor on the Flemish coast, the English navy effectively annihilated the French navy. There followed a succession of English incursions into French territory, leading to the famous major land battles at Crécy and Poitiers and to the smaller, less famous fights at Morlaix, Auberoche, and Mauron. At these battles, the chivalrous-warrior nobility of France displayed a tendency to treat battles as large-scale tournaments. The headlong frontal mass charge seemed to be the only tactic they understood. The French fell into a repeated pattern of being slaughtered by hailstorms of arrows from the massed longbows of English soldiers who were few in number, but professional in attitude. Time after time, the French fighting nobility seemed to prefer chasing personal glory to applying tactical common sense, and time after time they were unable or unwilling to coordinate with their common-born infantry, whether peasant levies or mercenary crossbowmen.[11] On the other side, the English fighting nobility habitually fought in disciplined close coordination with their common-born longbowmen.

After one of the several treaty-based truces that punctuated the Hundred Years' War, French military fortunes revived under the leadership of Bertrand du Guesclin. The pragmatic du Guesclin managed to subordinate French notions of chivalrous conduct to intelligent planning and execution. He followed a strategy of avoiding major battles while using clever maneuvering, raids, and sieges to take back much of the English-held lands in France between 1368 and 1380. Du Guesclin died in 1380, but sporadic minor fighting continued until 1396.[12] Another truce was in effect from 1396 to 1415.

King Henry V of England invaded France in 1415 in a campaign that climaxed at the Battle of Agincourt on October 25 of that year. It is worth digressing to describe the Battle of Agincourt at length in order to illuminate the magnitude of the military superiority that the English had established over the French by the time Joan came on the scene. Agincourt exemplified everything that was right with the English army and everything that was wrong with the French army for most of the Hundred Years' War.[13]

Henry's personal control of his well-disciplined army was absolute. He deployed his men for battle in a solid block formation that was about six men deep and about a thousand men abreast. The block of men thus had a depth of about six ranks and a breadth of about a thousand files. The thousand or so men of each rank stood shoulder-to-shoulder while the six or so men of each file stood one behind the other. This block of English fighting men stood in a flat, open, treeless farmer's field. However, Henry took pains to ensure that the extreme left and right ends ("flanks") of his block of men were each butted up against the large, thick forests that stood at each end of his army. European armies of that time were averse to fighting in forests because the close, irregularly placed trees would disrupt the close-packed shoulder-to-shoulder formations that European armies favored. By ensuring that both flanks of his army rested on large forests, Henry pre-

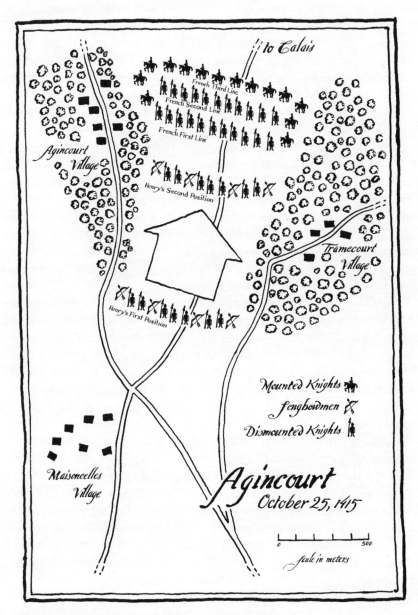

Map 3.1   Agincourt: October 25, 1415

vented the French from attacking in such a way as to curl around one or both of his flanks—thus collapsing his formation from the ends toward the middle. For a European-style army deployed in a broad shallow block, a powerful enemy attack enveloping an exposed flank was the catastrophic prelude to utter and bloody defeat. By securing his flanks on the forests, Henry guaranteed that any French attack on his position would have to come directly at him, frontally, face-to-face, straight into the teeth of his ready formation.

Henry subdivided his wide, shallow block of men into alternating subblocks of longbowmen and dismounted knights. Each subblock was shoulder-to-shoulder-contiguous with the adjacent blocks to its left and right—though of course, the far left and far right subblocks had their outer ends resting on the left and right forests respectively. Each subblock had the same six or so-man depth of the entire army block. Each subblock was several dozen men abreast. In the subblocks composed of longbowmen, the archers in the rear ranks could elevate the angle at which they shot in order to shoot their arrows safely over the heads of the archers in the front rank. (Some of the blocks of longbowmen, when viewed from above, were triangular rather than rectangular in shape, with the apex toward the French.)

The knights on both sides wore metal-plate armor with fully enclosed helmets and carried shields on their left arms while they gripped their swords or maces in their right hands.[14] Thus armed, the English knights would brawl with the oncoming French knights literally face-to-face. There is evidence that at least some of the French knights at Agincourt fought with shortened lances in lieu of swords.[15] The typical English longbowman was protected only by an open-faced metal helmet and by a vest covering his chest and back made of a combination of hard leather and chain mail.[16] The longbowmen relied on the ability of the armor-piercing arrows launched from their six-foot longbows to rain death on the French from a safe distance.[17] Additionally, every longbowman carried a six-foot-long wooden stake. Before battle, the longbowmen would hammer the stakes into the ground at a forty-five-degree angle and, using pruning knives, sharpen the ends that pointed toward the enemy. The longbowmen would place these stakes closely together to form a pointy hedge that was a precursor to barbed wire. They would then arrange themselves in their block formation, as previously described, immediately behind their protective hedge of stakes. Any group of French knights attempting to attack the longbowmen would first suffer under a hail of arrows as they tried to get close enough to hack at the weakly armored archers with their swords.

Upon reaching the hedge of stakes in front of the longbowmen, the reduced number of French knights who were still unwounded would then shy away from the stakes. These French knights would tend to shift laterally away from the longbowmen to fight face-to-face with the English knights who would be standing in block formations between the blocks of longbowmen.

The final and perhaps decisive strength of this English fighting system was that the noble-born English knights and the common-born English longbowmen respected each other's skill and courage and had long experience working together as a team. As day dawned on the field of Agincourt, Henry knew that this English fighting system in preceding decades had brought crushing victories over larger French armies at Crécy, Poitiers, and other places. He counted on this system to deliver victory once again.

The French army at Agincourt had over four times as many men as the English. But the French army was not really an army; it was a heterogeneous mob, whose weak leaders were incapable of imposing proper discipline. The noble French knights were individualistic glory seekers. As warriors, they were brave to the point of foolhardiness, as befitted their perception of themselves as paragons of chivalry. But when it came to matters of collective tactics and strategy, they were dilettantes. The French knights were augmented by foreign mercenary crossbowmen; but the knights scorned these crossbowmen, fellow soldiers in their own army, as social inferiors.[18]

The Battle of Agincourt began with the English drawn up in their formation in the field between the two forests. Less than a mile in front of the English, facing them from the opposite end of the alleyway between the two forests, the French arrayed themselves in three massive waves. Each wave was several men deep and over a thousand men abreast. Each wave contained more men than the entire English army. The French knights in the center of the first and second waves were on foot, while the knights on the left and right flanks of the first and second waves were on their horses. The entire third wave was on horseback.[19] There was some delay while the French knights brawled among themselves for the honor of standing in the front rank and thus being the first to cross swords with the English.[20]

Several hours passed while the French and English faced each other from opposite ends of the open field that lay between the forests. Each side wanted the other to attack first. Finally, Henry decided to force the issue. He ordered his longbowmen to pull up their protective hedge of stakes. Then, moving deliberately to stay neatly abreast of each other, the English knights and longbowmen marched toward the French. When his men came within distance of an extremely long longbow shot from the French, about 300 yards, Henry ordered his army to stop. He directed his archers to reinstall their hedge of stakes, which they hastily did. The English could just barely reach the French with their longbows, but they were still safely outside the range of the French crossbows. Henry ordered his longbowmen to shoot a salvo of arrows into the French, hoping to goad them into a frontal assault on his now firmly reestablished position.

Henry's gambit worked perfectly. Forgetting the lessons of Crécy and Poitiers, the French first wave surged forward, followed closely by the second. Because the distance between the forests was wider at the French end of the field than at the English end, the French found themselves crowded toward their center more and more as they ran toward the English. It had rained all the previous night, and the tightly packed French were soon panting for air as they slogged through the thick mud in their heavy armor. Now, stinging torrents of English arrows bit into the oncoming French. The French horses on the flanks went mad with pain from the arrows and trampled many of the French knights who were advancing on foot in the center. More French knights staggered and stumbled about in the mud to avoid the horses. When the exhausted and arrow-riddled French came to within sword's length of the English, they avoided the blocks of English longbowmen and crowded in toward the blocks of dismounted English knights. The haughty French knights saw no honor in grappling with lowborn archers. At last, the leading rank of French were able to fight like chivalrous nobles were supposed to fight—face-to-face with other nobles, swords swinging. The problem for the French was that they were badly winded by their jog through the mud and reeling from the arrows, while the English knights brawling with them were still fresh. Even worse, when the first rank of French clanged to a halt to duel with the English knights immediately in front of them, the dozens of following ranks of French continued to press forward; such was their frenzy to come to grips with the English. Because of this pressure from behind, the French knights in the first rank, who were actually crossing steel with the English knights, lost their ability to dodge and parry English blows. The first-rank French knights were pushed into the English swords by the force of their fellow Frenchmen shoving from behind. After the French first rank was slaughtered in this way, the second French rank became the new first rank and quickly met the same hideous fate. This process repeated itself unknown times in a cycle of butchery. In the horrific press of struggling bodies, scores of French knights toppled into the mud in their heavy armor, where they either drowned or were suffocated under the weight of more French falling on top of them. By now, the English longbowmen had run out of arrows. They threw down their longbows, drew out the long, narrow daggers they carried sheathed at their sides, and advanced forward, through and beyond their hedge of stakes. The lightly clad English archers, moving nimbly, set upon the immobilized and helpless French knights. These archers, who a short while before had written themselves off as dead men because of the overwhelming French numbers opposed to them, suddenly realized that they might not merely survive, but win. This sudden inversion of their emotional state probably made them go berserk. There followed a surreal nightmare of slaughter. The English archers' daggers could not punch through the metal plates of the French knights' armor. So, the English archers drove their daggers into the gaps in French armor at groin and armpit and into the eye slits of French helmets. Those English archers who were also armed with axes or mallets joined with their dagger-wielding fellows to assail exhausted, gasping French knights who could do nothing to save themselves. Meanwhile, the English knights continued to hack down the French knights who were directly in front of them.[21]

Agincourt became one of the most lopsided killing orgies in military history. English casualties were relatively light while the French were butchered in droves. The best modern estimate is that the English lost a few hundred men out of a starting strength of not quite 6,000 while the French lost almost 10,000 men out of a starting strength of over 24,000.[22] The entire French first wave was either killed or taken prisoner, as was much of the second. The French third wave watched in horror as the action unfolded and then retreated from the field, along with the survivors of the second wave. The flower of French chivalry was annihilated in less than an hour.

The Battle of Agincourt epitomized the recurring pattern of almost all the battles of the Hundred Years' War: English discipline and skill ruining mindless French valor and chivalrous pride. The result was ever-deepening despair in a French army that seemed incapable of learning from its mistakes. Any French leader who wanted to reverse the course of the war had to achieve the seeming miracle of overcoming both English strengths and French weaknesses. A leader who could achieve this seeming miracle was coming to the French, but on the day of Agincourt, she was still only about three years old.

In a series of campaigns following Agincourt, Henry conquered Normandy and established firm English rule over that region.[23] Now the Burgundians became major players in the war. The successive French-speaking dukes of Burgundy were ostensibly vassals of the successive kings of France, but the Burgundian dukes rivaled their masters in wealth and power. They were a vassal tail that wagged a sovereign dog. In the aftermath of Henry's victory at Agincourt, the Burgundians formed an alliance with the English and in 1418, the Burgundians took Paris.

King Charles VI of France signed the humiliating Treaty of Troyes with Henry in 1420. By the terms of the treaty, Charles married off his daughter Catherine to Henry. The firstborn son of this union would become the king of a united England and France. The son of Charles VI, the Dauphin Charles who had been in line to become Charles VII, was disinherited by the treaty. He fled to what was still so-called free France south of the Loire River and set up his court in the towns of Bourges and Chinon.

Desultory fighting continued and the so-called free French forces won a minor victory over the English at Baugé in 1421. In 1422, both Charles VI and Henry V died. Henry's infant son became King Henry VI of both England and France, with his uncle the duke of Bedford as regent. South of the Loire, the Dauphin Charles refused to accept the situation and continued the war as best he could. More French defeats followed at Cravant in 1423 and at Verneuil in 1424. At Verneuil, the French at last had the good sense to attempt a maneuver of envelopment against the exposed flanks of the English defenses, flanks that the English were unable to butt up against forests as they had done at Agincourt. But English discipline, effective English countermoves, the English longbow—and French despair—combined to give the Dauphin another defeat.

In the autumn of 1428, the English, later joined by the Burgundians, began their siege of the large city of Orléans. Orléans is situated immediately on the north bank of the Loire, and in 1428 it was one of the last pockets of free France left north of that river. The fall of the city seemed inevitable and the feeling on both sides of the war was that once the city fell, nothing could stop the English from driving into southern France and finishing things for good.

After decades of war, northern France was a devastated, depopulated shambles. Along the contested fringes of occupied and free France, lawlessness and brigandage were endemic. The villages in the contested regions lived a nightmare existence of fear. In one such village named Domrémy, a teenage girl contemplated the condition of her homeland in sorrow.

The English were having their problems too. The population and resource base of England were a fraction of those of France.[24] The English forces were stretched desperately thin on the ground to cover the parts of

France they had already conquered. They lacked sufficient men to conquer more. The apparently dominant position of the English was as much due to French despair as English prowess. All the French soldiers needed to turn the war around was a leader with the charisma to restore their spirits and the savvy to lead them properly.

Enter Joan.

Chapter 4

JOAN'S MILITARY CAREER: THE PRELIMINARIES

The purpose of this work is to describe, and, above all, to analyze Joan's military career. It is not meant to be a comprehensive biography narrating her entire life. Nonetheless, it is necessary to briefly outline Joan's early life and the means by which she came to be placed at the head of the army of France. The primary sources for information about Joan's childhood and initial rise to fame are her own testimony at her trial for heresy and the testimony of her friends, family members, and neighbors in her posthumous retrial. The story of how Joan rose from utter obscurity to a position of great influence has been retold so many times—in full-length biographies, in children's books, and in film—that it is almost common knowledge. What follows is a quick sketch of Joan's childhood, her initial rise to fame, and her first actions after she won for herself a position of influence.[1]

Joan (spelled "Jehanne" in fifteenth-century French) was born in the farm village of Domrémy in the eastern French frontier region of Lorraine. Her father was a peasant farmer named Jacques d'Arc and her mother was named Isabelle.[2] The date of her birth is traditionally given as January 6, the Feast of the Epiphany, 1412, but this date is based on flimsy evidence and hearsay that was current among Joan's admirers during her public career.[3] Like most peasants of her time, Joan was unsure of her own age. During her trial for heresy in 1431, she stated that her age was about nineteen, which would in fact put her birth in about 1412.[4]

Joan lived the childhood of an ordinary late-medieval peasant girl, receiving no formal education beyond her mother and her parish priest teaching her the rudiments of the Catholic faith. Her days were filled up with helping her mother spin thread, mend clothing, and cook, and with helping her father in the fields. Like all the other children in the village, she was periodically assigned duties of watching over grazing livestock and of herding the livestock from one pasture to another.

Domrémy was one of several villages and towns that comprised a small, isolated pocket of territory that was loyal to the Dauphin. This pocket of pro-Dauphin ground was completely surrounded by many miles of territory that supported the Burgundian faction. Given this situation, Joan was born and grew up in an environment where war was always close at hand and where the survival of her village was always precarious. Joan stated at her trial that one of her childhood duties was to help herd the village cattle to a relatively secure location in a nearby abandoned castle whenever hostile soldiers were rumored to be in the area.[5] In July 1428, when Joan was about sixteen, she, her family, and her neighbors had to flee to the town of Neufchâteau to escape a marauding force of Burgundians who menaced Domrémy. When the people of Domrémy were able to return home after a period of about two weeks, they found their houses burnt, their property plundered, and their village church gutted.[6] Joan's family was one of the most prosperous in the village. They lived in the only house in the village that was built of stone, not wood and thatch. Joan was thus fortunate that her house survived the Burgundian raid intact, but she must have been affected by the suffering of her now-homeless friends and neighbors.

As Joan herself testified at her trial, she had her first experience of receiving visions and hearing voices from heaven when she was about thirteen years of age. The voices were accompanied by a dazzling light and Joan, at first, "had great fear" of them. As the voices and visions came to her again and again over a period of time, Joan realized that they were benevolent and wanted to help her. She eventually identified the voices as those of Saint Catherine of Alexandria, Saint Margaret of Antioch, and Saint Michael, the warrior archangel. At first, testified Joan at her trial, the voices merely counseled her to be a good girl and to be faithful in her religious duties. It was around this time that Joan vowed to keep her virginity "for as long as it pleases God." Joan came to love the voices and to experience ecstasy when she heard them. As the years went by, the voices became evermore specific and insistent that Joan had been chosen by God to come to the aid of the long-suffering French people by leading the French army to victory over the English invaders and by helping the Dauphin to claim his rightful crown. Joan pleaded with her voices that she was "just a poor girl who knew nothing of riding and warfare," but they

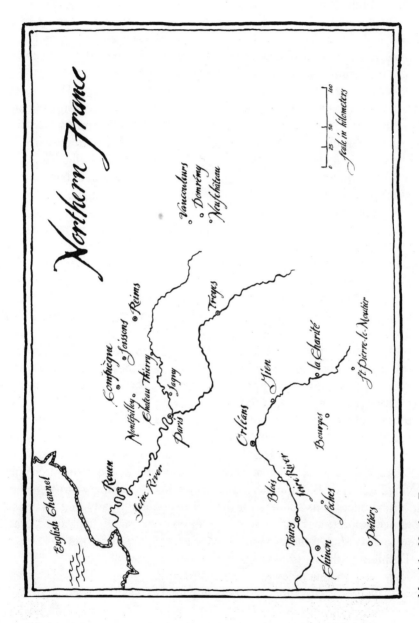

Map 4.1 Northern France

only increased their urgent insistence that she must leave Domrémy and journey to the Dauphin to offer her services.[7]

The administrative center of the pro-Dauphin enclave of which Domrémy was a part was located in the town of Vaucouleurs. A nobleman named Robert de Baudricourt commanded the garrison of Vaucouleurs. He was, in effect, the military governor of the small, isolated, pro-Dauphin region that included Domrémy. Joan claimed at her trial that her voices finally gave her specific orders to travel to Vaucouleurs. Her voices ordered her to petition de Baudricourt for an escort of armed men to conduct her through miles of hostile Burgundian territory and then to the Dauphin at his castle in the main part of free France.[8] Joan told no one in her family about either her voices or her mission from God. She made her first visit to Vaucouleurs in May 1428, when she was about sixteen. She told her parents that she was merely going to visit her cousin, who lived near Vaucouleurs, for a few days.[9]

After spending some days with her cousin, Joan revealed the true reason for her visit to her cousin's husband, a man named Durand Laxart. She importuned him to take her to the castle in Vaucouleurs and to request for her an audience with de Baudricourt so that she could petition him for help in her mission to save France. French folklore in Joan's time included several prophecies about a maiden from Lorraine who would save France in its most desperate days. These legendary prophecies were well known to French people of all social classes in Joan's day and were given considerable credence. Joan pointedly reminded Laxart of these prophecies when she asked his help in obtaining a hearing from de Baudricourt.[10] The obliging Laxart did as his young relative asked.

Escorted by Laxart, Joan apparently had no difficulty being admitted to the castle for an audience with de Baudricourt. Her problems started when she described her mission to de Baudricourt and asked him for an escort to the Dauphin. Prophecies or no prophecies about a maiden from Lorraine saving France, de Baudricourt roared with laughter, jokingly threatened to turn Joan over to his soldiers for their pleasure, and finally told Laxart to take her home to her father so he could box her ears.[11] Joan and Laxart were swiftly shown the way out of the castle. Joan returned to her family in Domrémy fully determined to pursue her mission.

Joan came to Vaucouleurs a second time in January 1429, when she was about seventeen. This time, she told her parents that she was going to help her cousin with housework during her cousin's pregnancy and that she would return home after her cousin gave birth. In fact, Joan would never see Domrémy again.[12]

JOAN'S MILITARY CAREER: THE PRELIMINARIES   29

Upon arriving in Vaucouleurs, Joan started a relentless campaign to obtain the backing she needed from de Baudricourt. Her repeated entreaties to de Baudricourt were met with repeated rebuffs, but still she did not lose heart. During one of her futile visits to de Baudricourt's castle, she was accosted in a jocular way by one of his knights, a man-at-arms named Jean de Metz, also known as Jean de Nouillompont. Years after the event, as he testified in her posthumous retrial, de Metz recalled his first conversation with Joan.

"My sweetie," de Metz said to Joan, "What are you doing here? Mustn't the king be driven from his kingdom and all of us become English?" According to de Metz, Joan responded by launching into a speech that was strident but eloquent. She was to make many such speeches in her career, but her verbal eruption at de Metz was the first such speech to be remembered by one of her associates and the first to be set down for posterity. She began by venting her frustration that de Baudricourt had again refused to provide her with an armed escort to the Dauphin. Nonetheless, she declared, she must journey to the Dauphin "even if I have to wear my legs down to the knees" with walking to his castle. Joan next displayed her awareness of dynastic politics when she declared that not even the recent betrothal of a Scottish princess to the Dauphin's son could rescue the kingdom of France. Only she herself, peasant girl Joan, could bring help to the kingdom, she forcefully insisted. She lamented having to leave her poor mother, but since her sire had commanded her to save France, she had to obey. When de Metz asked her who her sire was, she declared that her Sire was God. According to de Metz, he then placed his hands in Joan's hands and vowed that, with the help of God, he would help her reach the Dauphin. Joan had made her first convert. De Metz next asked Joan when she wanted to be on her way. "Better today than tomorrow, better tomorrow than the day after," she replied.[13]

It was not going to be quite that easy. De Baudricourt still had to be won over. But now, at least, one of de Baudricourt's key subordinates was earnestly in Joan's camp and could be counted on to argue in her favor. Also, by now, Joan had become quite a celebrity in Vaucouleurs.[14] The popular prophecies about the maiden from Lorraine saving France were doing their work and the townspeople were becoming increasingly vocal in their support for Joan.

By the time that Joan was making her case in Vaucouleurs, it had become common knowledge all over France that the English had laid siege to Orléans and that the situation of that city was becoming increasingly desperate. On February 12, 1429, the English inflicted yet another crushing defeat on the French army in a battle fought in the open field at

Rouvray, not far from Orléans. According to one story that is probably apocryphal, Joan confronted de Baudricourt on February 12 and told him that at that moment, the French were suffering a severe defeat near Orléans—this when the fastest means of communication was a messenger on horseback and when Orléans was several days' hard ride from Vaucouleurs. De Baudricourt dismissed her words out of hand, so the story goes, only to be stunned several days later when a messenger arrived to confirm Joan's clairvoyant knowledge of events taking place far away.[15]

According to accounts that are probably *not* apocryphal, what de Baudricourt did do shortly after the Battle of Rouvray was order a priest to perform an exorcism on Joan to see if she was possessed by evil spirits. Joan passed this test in grand fashion, proving her purity and sanctity to the satisfaction of everyone involved.[16] Shortly after this event, de Baudricourt at last relented. He agreed to provide Joan with an armed escort of six men, including Jean de Metz and a squire named Bertrand de Poulengy.[17]

De Metz and de Poulengy, assisted by some citizens of Vaucouleurs, provided Joan with the male clothing she requested.[18] For her own part, she cropped her hair short and round in the male fashion of the time. She was also provided with a horse of her own so she could keep up with her six horse-mounted escorts. For someone who had protested to her voices that she was "just a poor girl who knew nothing of riding," her equestrian skills seem to have been superb.[19]

On February 23, 1429, the little party set out on the arduous and perilous journey to the Dauphin's castle at Chinon. They would have to ride across 350 miles of France, much of it through hostile Burgundian territory. The people of Vaucouleurs turned out to give Joan and her escorts an emotional sendoff. De Baudricourt went so far as to present her with a sword as a gift. As Joan and her companions prepared to ride out of the west gate of Vaucouleurs toward their destiny, de Baudricourt spoke his parting words to her: "Go, go—and come what may."[20]

Rather miraculously, the group made its way to Chinon without any serious trouble. While they were traversing Burgundian territory, they rode at night and laid low during the day. They arrived at Chinon on March 6. The Dauphin and his court were well aware of Joan's approach. While she was traveling through friendly territory on the last leg of her journey to Chinon, Joan had dictated a letter to a scribe, addressed to Charles, announcing her desire to meet with him. A messenger rode ahead of Joan and her party at speed to deliver the letter to Chinon.[21] Even without this letter, the news of Joan and her mission had spread across France with remarkable rapidity. Even the commander of the French forces defending the besieged city of Orléans heard the news about Joan. He took the step of sending two emissaries to infiltrate through the English forces and go on to Chinon to obtain more information about this remarkable girl.[22] It seems obvious that the old prophecies about a maiden from Lorraine saving France were doing their work by preparing Joan's way for her.

After Joan arrived in Chinon, the Dauphin Charles grievously tried her patience by making her wait for two or three days while his advisors debated whether or not he should receive her. A small panel of Charles's advisors questioned Joan, without Charles present, in order to determine the advisability of allowing her to meet the Dauphin. A critical factor in her favor was the arrival of the messenger that de Baudricourt had sent to Charles by a separate route, carrying de Baudricourt's written endorsement of her mission.[23] Charles eventually decided to see her and sent word down into the town of Chinon ordering Joan to present herself to him at the castle.

Photo 4.1 This period German tapestry depicts Joan arriving at the castle of Chinon for her first meeting with the Dauphin Charles. The makers of the tapestry erroneously show Joan as already having her suit of armor and famous banner at this early point in her career. The fact that this tapestry was made in Germany shortly after Joan's lifetime demonstrates how quickly and how widely her story resonated across Europe. © The Art Archive / The Art Archive.

At the appointed time, Joan strode into the great hall of the royal castle of Chinon. The huge room was filled with dozens of lords and ladies, all of them wearing their court finery. One can only imagine their whispered comments to each other as they beheld a robustly healthy peasant girl, with her hair cut short and wearing a man's clothes, walking among them. According to various accounts, Charles sought to test Joan's divine gift of clairvoyance. He wore clothing that was plainer than that of many of his courtiers and he hid himself among the throng of people crowding the hall. One account even claims that he ordered an impostor to sit on his throne. Charles reasoned that if Joan were truly sent by God, she would be able to pick him out of the crowd. If she were a false prophet, then she would be deceived as to who was really Charles in the great hall. Joan passed her test in stunning fashion. She picked Charles out of the crowd, stood before him, and curtsied, even while wearing male clothing. She then addressed him as "gentle Dauphin," proclaimed herself to be Joan the Maiden, and announced to him her mission to see him crowned the rightful king of France. Even when Charles attempted to prolong his deception by denying that he was the Dauphin, Joan refused to be fooled, saying to Charles "it is you and none other." Joan's tour de force performance created an instantaneous sensation among the assembled courtiers.[24]

One should not make too much of Joan's ability to pick Charles out of the crowd. Before she entered the great hall, Joan would have had many opportunities to pump knowledgeable people for information about Charles, including what he looked like. Charles's stooped posture, knock-knees, shuffling walk, large nose, and small, squinty eyes made him easily recognizable.[25]

Joan and Charles drew apart from the crowd and held a prolonged and intense conversation out of everyone's earshot. By the end of this conversation, Charles was almost, but not quite totally, convinced that Joan was the solution to his and France's problems. Generations of scholars have speculated about what words passed between Joan and Charles to win him over. We will never know.[26] The most immediate result of the conversation was that Charles ordered that Joan be moved out of her room at the inn located in the town of Chinon and that she take up residence in Chinon castle as his honored guest.[27]

The next day, Joan had her first meeting with the man who would become her most significant comrade in arms during her military career. The young and handsome Jean, Duke of Alençon, was a kinsman of the Dauphin Charles and one of the leading nobles of the realm. As soon as he heard the news about the remarkable farm girl who had announced her

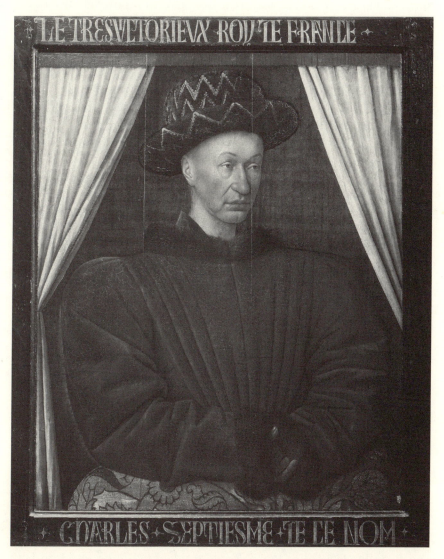

Photo 4.2 As shown with almost brutal frankness by the painter Jean Fouquet, Charles was a feeble physical specimen, even in his youth. His uninspiring physical presence matched his weakness of character. He would be brought to his rightful crown by the efforts of loyal subjects who were stronger in both body and spirit than he. After the successful conclusion of the Hundred Years' War, Charles had coins minted bearing his profile and the motto "Charles the Victorious." Among his more astute subjects, he was known as "Charles the Well Served." © The Art Archive / Musèe du Louvre Paris / Dagli Orti.

intention to save France, he had come to Chinon of his own accord for the express purpose of meeting her. Joan and d'Alençon took an immediate and profound liking to each other that would only grow stronger as time passed. On being introduced to d'Alençon, Joan told him, "It is good that you have come! The more royal blood of France is brought together, the better." For his part, d'Alençon was deeply impressed by Joan's superb natural skills with a horse and lance as he watched her practice jousting at a target.[28]

Charles and the regime he headed still needed more proof that Joan was in fact on a mission from God, not from the Devil. To obtain this proof, Joan was conveyed to the city of Poitiers to undergo three weeks of questioning by a panel of eighteen theologians and learned churchmen.[29] These men asked Joan many probing and sophisticated questions on points of Christian faith. They found themselves astonished by both the confidence and the wisdom of the illiterate peasant girl's answers. Joan won new supporters with every answer she gave during these proceedings. Even so, the delay that the days of questioning imposed on her plans to place herself at the head of the army and march to the rescue of Orléans grated on her nerves. When one of the learned clerics told Joan that the panel could not advise the Dauphin to entrust his army to her based on just her assurances, that they needed some sort of sign from her, Joan's reply must have been dangerously close to an impertinent shout: "In God's name, I did not come to Poitiers to make signs; but send me to Orléans, and there I will make the signs for which I was sent." The churchmen apparently took no offense at this bold reply, but rather took it as more evidence of Joan's seriousness of purpose. At the end of the three weeks of questioning, the clerics reported to Charles that Joan was a good and true Christian acting on noble motives, and that he would do well to accept her help in conducting the war.[30]

Charles and his advisors required another form of proof that Joan's inspiration was divine, not diabolical. According to the beliefs of the time, a woman became a witch by having sexual intercourse with either Satan or one of his demons. Joan had to endure not one, but two, intrusive physical examinations by ladies of the royal court to confirm that she was a female and a virgin. The ladies found Joan's maidenhead to be intact on both occasions and duly reported to Charles that she could never have consorted with the Devil and his minions.[31]

While Joan was submitting herself to examinations both intellectual and physical, she also took action of her own to advance her program for France. She dictated a letter addressed to the highest-ranking leaders of the English forces in France that must rate as one of the most ringing ultimatums in history:

JESUS-MARY

King of England, and you, Duke of Bedford who call yourself Regent of the Kingdom of France; and you, William de la Pole, Earl of Suffolk; John, Lord Talbot; and you, Thomas, Lord of Scales who call yourselves lieutenants of the said Duke of Bedford, act with reason toward the King of Heaven; surrender to the Maid, who is sent here by God, the King of Heaven, the keys of all the good towns you have taken and violated in France. She is come from God to uphold the blood royal. She is completely ready to make peace if you will come to reason with her, by leaving France and paying for what you have taken. And among you, archers, men-at-arms, gentlemen and others who are before the city of Orléans, go back into your own country, by God; and if you do not do so, wait for news of the Maid, who will see you shortly, to your very great damage. King of England, if you do not do so, I am Chief of War, and in whatever place that I find your people in France, I will make them leave it, willingly or unwillingly. And if they will not obey, I will have them all killed; I am sent by God, the King of Heaven to, body for body, drive them out of all France. And if they obey, I will give them mercy. And do not have another opinion, for you do not hold the Kingdom of France from God, the King of Heaven, son of Saint Mary; it will be held by King Charles, the true heir; for God, the King of Heaven, wills it, and so it is revealed by the Maid; who will enter Paris with a good company. If you will not believe this news from God and the Maid, in whatever place we find you, we will strike with such a great *hahay* as has not been in France for a thousand years, if you do not come to reason. And believe firmly that the King of Heaven will send more force to the Maid than you can lead in all your assaults against her and her good men-at-arms; and on the horizon it will be seen who has the better right from the King of Heaven. You, Duke of Bedford, the Maid begs and requires of you that you do not cause your own destruction. If you will be reasonable, you may yet come into her company, where the French will do the greatest feat ever done for Christianity. And make response if you want to make peace in the city of Orléans; and if you do not, think of the great damage that will come to you quickly. Written this Tuesday of Holy Week.[32]

The audacity of a simple farm girl in making such demands, in such a tone, to mighty paladins, remains amazing to this day. It is interesting to note that when Joan invited Bedford to join her to watch the French perform the greatest feat ever for Christianity, she was apparently inviting him to join her in a new crusade to free the Holy Land from the Saracens. The record of history is not clear whether this letter was delivered to the English high command before Joan arrived at Orléans, or concurrently with her arrival there.[33]

It was during this phase of her career that Joan provided history with the most unambiguous evidence of her gift for prophecy. In the archives today, there is an official letter, written by a Flemish envoy who worked in the French city of Lyon, dated April 22, 1429 and addressed to his superiors in Brussels. This letter records that Joan had made a public prophecy that she would be wounded in the fighting at Orléans, but that she would not be killed. The most important day of fighting at Orléans was May 7, 1429—and on that day, Joan suffered the most severe of the several wounds she would receive during her career as a soldier. She is thus officially on record as making a prophecy that came true in about fifteen days.[34]

Having passed every form of examination that could be devised, having finally proven to the leadership of France that she was precisely what she claimed herself to be, Joan's next important stop was the city of Tours. In Tours she was measured and fitted for a custom-made suit of armor. Her armor was described as "white," not because it was literally white, but because it was plain, bare metal, without heraldic ornamentation. For that reason, her armor must have shone all the brighter in the sun. Also in Tours, Joan commissioned the sewing and painting of the enormous personal banner that she would carry into battle throughout her military career. Additionally, she ordered a smaller, personal pennant for herself.[35]

Charles had already officially conferred upon Joan the title "chief of war." This title was deliberately vague as to where it placed Joan in the command hierarchy of the French army.[36] Joan took charge of the official military entourage that Charles and other members of the regime provided for her. This entourage included two squires, two pages, two heralds (messengers), a personal priest, and a treasurer, as was fitting for a war leader of great prestige. Two other members of her entourage were none other than her brothers Pierre and Jean, who had journeyed all the way from Domrémy to join her in the struggle to liberate France.[37] Like Joan, they were equipped for war at public expense.

Now that she was completely outfitted as a warrior leader, Joan and her entourage traveled to the city of Blois, where the army of France was assembling to go to the rescue of Orléans. About 4,000 men would march with Joan to that beleaguered city.[38] D'Alençon's administrative talents were needed to oversee the gathering of more troops and supplies. He would stay behind and miss out on this particular expedition.[39]

On April 27, 1429, Joan and the army set out from Blois on the road to Orléans. Priests marched at the head of the column, singing hymns as they went.

Chapter 5

JOAN'S ACHIEVEMENT IN RAISING FRENCH MORALE: THE FIRST PART OF "WHAT"

To find the truth about Joan's military qualities, it is necessary to turn to the testimony given at her retrial by the soldiers who knew her. The military men who dealt intimately with Joan on a daily basis during her campaigns and whose reminiscences were recorded in the documents of the retrial were several. The two highest-ranking of them were Jean, duke of Alençon, who became Joan's key adherent at Chinon, and Jean, count of Dunois. Dunois was the illegitimate half-brother of the duke of Orléans. Until he received the title of "count of Dunois" later in life, his proper title was "Bastard of Orléans." In the vague and imprecise military organization of late medieval France, the Bastard and d'Alençon may be understood as Joan's co-commanders of the army at war. Other witnesses were members of Joan's personal entourage. Jean d'Aulon was her squire while young Louis de Coutes was her page. Brother Jean Pasquerel was her personal priest and confessor. Jean de Metz and Bertrand de Poulengy, Joan's original companions on the journey from Vaucouleurs to Chinon, also gave key testimony at the retrial.[1]

The firsthand sources make clear that the most obvious and stunning impact of Joan's leadership was the way in which her charismatic personality lifted the morale of the often-defeated French army. She raised them up from the pit of cynicism and despair to a fevered high of renewed enthusiasm and collective ardor for battle. Conversely, once her reputation for bringing victory to the French became established, her presence infected the heretofore invincible English with doubt and fear. The Bastard testified as follows about Joan's impact from the moment she sent her ultimatum to the English army besieging Orléans:

> That letter [Joan's ultimatum] was sent to Lord Talbot [commander of English forces at Orléans]...before...the English, in the number of two hundred, would put to flight eight hundred or a thousand men of the royal army, from that moment four or five hundred men of the king could give battle against almost all the English forces.[2]

Jean de Wavrin was a Burgundian officer who fought against Joan as an ally of the English. He wrote a chronicle titled *Recueil de chroniques et anchiennes istoires de la Grant Bretaigne a present nommee Engleterre*.[3] He stated, "By the renown of Joan the Maid, the English courage was greatly impaired and fallen off. They saw...their fortune turn her wheel rudely contrary to them...by the enterprises of the said Maid."[4] A high-ranking English leader, the duke of Gloucester, twice felt compelled to issue written orders disciplining English soldiers who refused to take ship for France or who had deserted out of terror of Joan's apparent, to them, use of sorcery.[5] The strongest piece of evidence regarding Joan's disastrous impact on the will of the English to fight is a letter written by the duke of Bedford. Bedford was the English regent ruling occupied France in the name of his nephew, the boy-king Henry VI. Writing to the English council in 1433, two years after Joan's death, he bemoaned the reverses to English arms that began with Joan's appearance at the siege of Orléans in 1429:

> And alle thing there prospered for you, til the tyme of the siege of Orleans taken in hand, God knoweth by what advis. At the whiche tyme, after the adventure fallen to the persone of my cousin of Salysbury, whom God assoille, there felle, by the hand of God, as it seemeth, a greet strook upon your peuple that was assembled there in grete nombre, caused in grete partie, as y trowe, of lakke of sadde beleve, and of unlevefulle doubte that thei hadde of a disciple and lyme of the Feende, called the Pucelle, ["the Maiden," Joan's self-chosen title] that used fals enchauntements and sorcerie. The which strooke and discomfiture nought oonly lessed in grete partie the nombre of youre people, there, but as well withdrowe the courage of the remenant in merveillous wyse, and couraiged youre adverse partie and ennemys to assemble hem forthwith in grete nombre.[6]

After calling Joan the disciple and limb of the Devil, Bedford blamed her false enchantments and sorcery for killing many English and demoralizing the rest. Finally, he cited the courage she brought to England's enemies, leading the French to gather in great numbers behind her.

Joan had to start with the little things and work up to the big things in her drive to restore the fighting spirit of the French. When she first joined the army, she did not have any practical rank or authority with which to compel obedience. Though she was resplendent astride her horse in her new armor, carrying her new banner made to her order, she was, at that point, only under the escort of the officers who had real powers of command. However, she immediately set about making the force of her personality felt throughout the army in terms of both morals and morale. She continued to stress the importance of righteous conduct of the soldiers throughout her career. As Brother Pasquerel, de Coutes, d'Alençon, and others testified, she exhorted the soldiers to become faithful in making confession and attending mass, she drove prostitutes from camp brandishing her sword, and she fiercely scolded both common soldiers and great nobles for their foul language. To their own amazement, hardened warriors of all ranks meekly submitted to her will in these matters.[7] George Bernard Shaw was correct when he wrote in the preface to his play *Saint Joan* that what may seem to be nothing more than mere prudery on Joan's part was in fact a vital component of restoring the ability of the French army to fight well. Soldiers of all ranks had become so cynical, so demoralized by alternating periods of defeat and inaction, that they were ready to accept *any* measures that would restore a modicum of their self-respect. Joan's exhortations on little points such as attending mass and avoiding blasphemy were the necessary first steps in rebuilding the men's spirits.[8]

Joan's insistence on high moral standards in her army created complications in the practical conduct of her military campaigns. Armies on both sides of the Hundred Years' War typically plundered the communities through which they marched for food. Joan's absolute moral prohibition of this practice made her army's supply problems more difficult, especially during the march on Reims to have Charles crowned. According to an eyewitness story told at her retrial, she once tried to slap one of her soldiers who, she discovered, had served her a meal in the field that the soldier had made from plundered food.[9] Joan's prohibition on plundering also had a practical benefit in the context of the overall conduct of the war. Joan's ultimate objective was to unite the people of France in willing loyalty to Charles, their king. To achieve this objective, it was essential for her to wage war on Charles's behalf in such a way as to earn the goodwill of the people. By forbidding her army to plunder, she did much to gain this popular goodwill.

Jane Marie Pinzino, in her unpublished manuscript titled "Just War, Joan of Arc and the Politics of Salvation," points out that Joan, knowingly or unknowingly, conducted herself according to the long-established doctrines of "just war."[10] As Pinzino describes, the doctrines of moral right conduct by combatants in war were first clearly enunciated by Augustine of Hippo in the early Middle Ages. Augustine's theories of what constituted just war were amplified in the fourteenth century by authors such as Giovanni da Legnano and Honoré Bonet.

Da Legnano's book, *Tractatus de Bello, de Represaliis et de Duello* (Tractate on War, Reprisals, and the Duel), and Bonet's book, *Arbre des batailles* (The Tree of Battles), were both voluminous and detailed instruction manuals on the rules that soldiers and commanders had to follow if they were to conduct war in accordance with the principles of justice.[11] In a sense, both these books were forerunners of the Geneva Conventions of our own time.

Pinzino argues that Joan adhered to three of the key moral principles established by Augustine, da Legnano, and Bonet in the way she conducted her part of the Hundred Years' War. First, Joan secured permission to wage war from a legitimate authority, in her case, the Dauphin Charles. Second, she fought in a war of self-defense, not in a war of conquest. Third, she sent ultimatums to her English enemies, offering them the chance to leave France in peace, before she made active war against them. Pinzino points out that whether or not uneducated Joan learned about just-war theory from her well-educated cohorts, she conducted herself as if she were well-versed in just-war theory.[12] In so doing, she lent credibility to the idea that she was fighting for a righteous cause, thereby boosting her prestige in the eyes of her supporters.

In their respective books, both da Legnano and Bonet included a very few pages offering practical advice for military commanders on how to win.[13] Just as Geoffroi de Charny did in his treatise on chivalry, da Legnano and Bonet devoted a scant number of pages to the practical aspects of war-fighting while providing their readers with hundreds of pages on the moral rules that military leaders were expected to follow. This suggests that the medieval Western European conception of the ideal military commander placed far greater stress on the commander's moral qualities than on his technical competence in planning and fighting battles. If this is so, then Joan's conspicuously high moral standards in leading her army helped her conform to the ideal image of a military commander of her day, even if her technical expertise in the conduct of war may have been a bit thin. Joan's conspicuous display of the moral rectitude expected of a military leader of her time can only have helped to solidify the loyalty of her common soldiers and the respect of the great nobles who were her putative peers in leading the army.

From the moment she first rode onto a battlefield, Joan went far beyond being merely the tireless good conscience of the army. From the moment she first laid eyes on her country's English enemies, she aroused the will of her soldiers to *fight*. Joan was a fine and forceful speaker, but her ability to inspire the French soldiers stemmed from her leading them into battle in the most literal sense possible. She was in the front rank of every assault that she ordered to be launched. The fighting men who knew her testified to this repeatedly. D'Aulon recounted that at the battle fought outside the English fort of the Augustins, near Orléans, the French were withdrawing unmolested back to Orléans when the English suddenly appeared to attempt a surprise attack on the rear of the French column. Joan arrived on the scene just at that moment, accompanied by the redoubtable French captain known as La Hire. Both of them were on horseback, armed with lances. Joan, with only La Hire at her side, immediately and impetuously leveled her lance and charged headlong at the English. D'Aulon said that she and La Hire struck the first blows at the enemy. The French knights and common soldiers, stung to action by Joan's example, turned about and swept the English from the field. They went on to storm the Augustins that day, giving Joan another victory.[14] Sadly for historians, La Hire died before Joan's retrial began. His testimony would have been invaluable.[15]

D'Alençon testified that during the assault on the walled town of Jargeau, Joan was one of the first to mount a scaling ladder set against the wall, shouting encouragement to her men as she did so. During earlier fighting in the outskirts of Jargeau, said d'Alençon, the French were being pushed back until Joan rode up, brandishing her banner, and led the men forward to successfully renew the attack.[16] Joan herself stated at her trial for heresy that she was the first to set a scaling ladder against the wall of the English fort of the Tourelles, outside of Orléans.[17] Even Georges Chastellain, a chronicler of the Burgundians, the French faction allied to the English who fought *against* Joan, was moved to praise her courage and personal example. During the hasty French retreat from a Burgundian ambush outside of Compiègne, Joan, in the last moments before she was taken prisoner, stayed behind with the rear guard so that her men could make good their escape. Chastellain recorded that she, "passing the nature of women, took all the brunt, and took many pains to save her company, remaining behind as chief and the most valiant of her troop."[18] Within minutes, Joan was bodily pulled off her horse by swarming Burgundian soldiers. It is remarkable that the chronicler of her foes would accord her such honor in his account of her last battle.

Even if Joan's military role was nothing more than that of a cheerleader, she was a cheerleader of superb tenacity and fortitude. As overlapping testimonies by the Bastard, d'Aulon, de Coutes, and Brother Pasquerel relate, she was shot through her shoulder by an English arrow at the Tourelles outside Orléans.[19] D'Alençon described how she was hit on her helmet by a thrown stone at Jargeau.[20] D'Alençon's personal chronicler, Perceval de Cagny, recorded that she was shot through her thigh by another arrow at Paris.[21] In every case, she ardently continued the fight despite her pain. At the Tourelles, the French became disheartened and the English emboldened when they saw Joan, conspicuous with her plain but shining armor and large banner, hit by the arrow and evacuated from the field. But when both sides saw Joan return to the front ranks a short time later with her wound staunched, waving her banner with her good arm and shouting for one more effort, the morale of the French soared while that of the English plummeted. The Bastard testified that the moment she returned to the fight, "the English trembled with fear; the soldiers of the king regained courage."[22] De Coutes said that the English "were terrified...in that last attack or last assault, the English made no defense."[23]

Intangible moral factors are of consummate importance on the field of battle. The soldiers' will to fight, or lack of it, often means more than numbers, weapons technology, or tactics in determining the outcome. Joan's moral impact in favor of the French and against the English was immediate and unmistakable. Her effect on the soldiers who could see or hear her was obvious.

Equally obvious was Joan's uplifting impact on the spirits of the French people of both sexes and all social classes in those parts of the realm loyal to Charles. Her sudden and astonishing appearance on the stage made a broken and despondent people believe with equal suddenness that they could reverse the calamities of decades of war by following where she pointed the way. She became the living, walking, speaking, *fighting* talisman of hope for a people who had lost hope. To her own sincere ill-ease, she became the focus of a personality cult that followed her wherever she went. Whenever the itinerary of Joan's short but intense career took her to a town of any size, the townspeople typically went into a frenzy of public adoration for her. Her progress through the streets was continually impeded by loving crowds who mobbed her, each person in the crowd pressing forward to touch her or even just her horse.[24] In keeping with the intense piety of the age, the people regarded Joan as if she were an angel sent to them in their time of distress.

This public mass adoration of Joan became translated into a practical military result in the form of recruitment for the army.[25] Before Joan, Charles's army had consisted of such meager and demoralized loyal troops and mercenaries as Charles could afford to maintain with his pitiful finances. With the advent of Joan, fighting men of all social classes suddenly came in droves, of their own accord, to follow her banner, serving at their own expense if need be. Perceval de Cagny wrote in his chronicle that Charles had no money to pay the army; nonetheless, nobles and commoners of all ranks "did not refuse to go serve the king for that journey in the Maid's company, saying that they would go everywhere she wanted to go."[26] A young French knight named Guy de Laval wrote a letter home to his mother saying that in the army "nor ever did men go with a better will to a task than they go to this one." He went on to tell his mother to sell and mortgage his lands if need be to raise money for the cause.[27] Clearly, Joan's moral inspiration turned an army of sullen mercenaries into a cross-social class army of crusaders.[28] It was an army that ostensibly belonged to Charles but that in its soul belonged to Joan.

Joan's moral impact, both in arousing the will of the French soldiers—of all social ranks—to fight, and in igniting a new blaze of hope in the French people loyal to Charles, was the one quality of hers that did the most to change history. In a few days at Orléans, she inverted what had been the established moral order on the battlefields of the Hundred Years' War. She made an army of habitual losers believe in themselves as winners. For the French army with Joan, the belief in victory and the fact of victory became mutually reinforcing. Renewed belief in victory brought with it a new will to fight and the will to fight brought the first victories; and those victories stoked an ever-hotter will to fight. Only the folly of Charles in freezing his victorious army in place while he carried on fruitless negotiations, only his shortsightedness in disbanding his army at the height of its power, broke the cycle of belief and victory that Joan had started.

Chapter 6

JOAN'S ACHIEVEMENT AS A MILITARY COMMANDER: THE SECOND PART OF "WHAT"

JOAN'S INITIAL TIME OF MILITARY SUCCESS

Joan's military role as an inspiring creator of the will to fight is obvious and indisputable. Establishing to what degree she was more than just a "super cheerleader"—to what degree she was a true commander who made decisions and gave orders concerning the strategic and tactical conduct of the war—is much more problematic. What complicates this question is that the French army of Joan's day had nothing that modern military professionals would call a chain of command. Whether it was a case of strategic decisions made at the royal court, or of tactical decisions made in a tent in the field, decisions seem to have been made in an extremely loose committee fashion, with the most forceful speaker present able to make his *or her* view carry the others along.[1] These ad hoc "committees," to use a modern term, could consist of the Dauphin-King and a mix of more or less coequal court nobles, warrior nobles, and captains of independent bands—plus a new, unprecedented, explosive factor in the person of Joan. As before, the testimony given in Joan's retrial must be the foundation of any effort to grasp the truth of the situation.

In the retrial, Simon Charles, who served as president of the chamber of accounts to Dauphin and King Charles VII, and who accompanied the army on the march to Reims, testified that "Joan was very simple in all her actions, except in war, in which she was very expert."[2] A knight named Thibault d'Armagnac stated:

> Apart from the doings of war, she was simple and innocent; but, in the moving and disposition of troops, in the doings of war and in the organization of combat and encouraging the troops, she behaved like she was the most skillful captain in the world, trained in all times for war.[3]

D'Alençon testified:

> Apart from making war, Joan's behavior was simple and young; but for war she was very skilled, both in carrying a lance, in assembling the army, in organizing for combat, and in placing the artillery. Everyone was full of admiration that she behaved with skillfulness and prudence in military actions, like she was a captain who had been making war for twenty or thirty years, and especially in the placing of artillery, in which she excelled.[4]

These general comments find backing in specific instances of Joan's words and deeds.

Joan made her debut as a warrior leader in the series of battles that broke the English siege of the city of Orléans. It is necessary to digress at some length to describe the military situation at Orléans as it existed the day before Joan arrived. In 1429, Orléans had a population of about 30,000 people.[5] Prior to Joan's arrival, about 2,000 fighting men of various types and ranks defended the city. In addition to these roughly 2,000 regular soldiers, there may have been as many as 3,000 militiamen drawn from the city's civil population, but these would have been of dubious military value.[6]

Like most major cities of its day, Orléans was protected by high, castle-like walls that completely enclosed the city. At intervals along the walls were towers capable of serving as platforms for various stone-throwing engines of war, such as traditional catapults, and for newer weapons, specifically, gunpowder cannons. With these weapons mounted in their towers, the defenders of Orléans could shoot back at the English besiegers who were bombarding the city with catapults and cannons of their own. Also located at intervals along the city walls were strongly built and heavily guarded gateways that provided entry to, and exit from, the city in times of peace. The city of Orléans was sited on the north bank of the Loire River. The walls on the south side of the city, the side that bordered the river, went right down to the water's edge.

Orléans was connected to the south bank of the Loire by an impressive multi-arch stone bridge that spanned the river. On the northern end, that is, the Orléans end of the bridge, a fortified gate pierced the city walls to provide peacetime access to the city for traffic on the bridge. At the southern end of the bridge, that is, on the opposite end of the bridge from the city, a set of huge, stone, castlelike towers straddled the bridge's southernmost pier. These towers were called the Tourelles. The purpose of these towers was to provide early warning for the city's defenders and to prevent any foe from setting foot on the bridge and then attacking over the bridge to menace the southern, riverside wall of the city. A heavy wooden drawbridge, which could be raised in times of danger, connected the Tourelles to the south bank of the river.

The Loire River flows generally from east to west across the approximate middle of France. By 1429, virtually all of France north of the Loire was under English or Burgundian occupation. For both sides in the war, the city of Orléans possessed tremendous psychological and strategic importance because it was one of the last patches of free French territory left north of the Loire. If the English could capture Orléans, the city, together with its bridge, would provide them with the ideal springboard for attacks aimed at the heart of free France, south of the river.

An English army appeared before the walls of Orléans to commence siege operations on October 12, 1428. The English were later joined in their siege by an allied Burgundian contingent. However, a falling out between the duke of Burgundy and the English regent in France, the duke of Bedford, led to the Burgundian contingent quitting the siege and marching away shortly before Joan arrived.[7] By the time Joan came to Orléans, after the city had been under siege for over six months, the number of English soldiers present was probably a little in excess of 4,000 men.[8]

The Englishmen's most important success during the siege occurred when they captured the Tourelles from the French and made that vital fortified position their own. The English also demolished two arches of the bridge near the Tourelles. The French countered by breaking down an arch near the middle of the bridge.[9] The loss of the Tourelles was a potentially fatal blow to the defenders of Orléans. By taking the Tourelles, the English cut the city off from direct access to supplies and reinforcements coming from free France.

With only about 4,000 English soldiers present, plus about 1,500 allied Burgundians, the English simply did not have enough men to put them shoulder-to-shoulder all the way around Orléans. Instead, they grouped their men in small forts that were scattered in a huge circle around the city.[10] By the time Joan arrived at Orléans, the English had built eleven of these forts. Some of the English forts were built of earth and timber from the ground up; other forts were preexisting French structures that the English had captured and then augmented with earth and timber additions. Prominent among the forts in the second category was the Tourelles. In

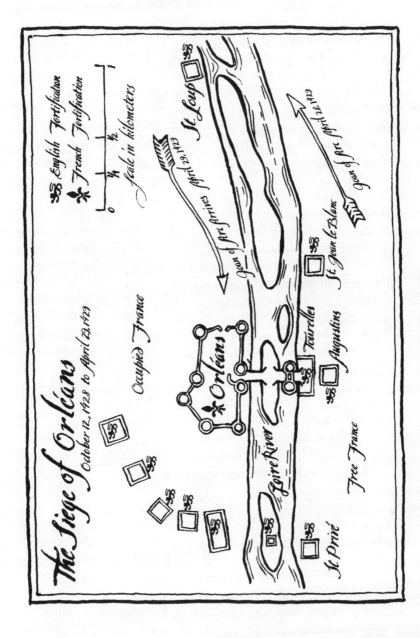

Map 6.1 The Siege of Orléans: October 12, 1428 to April 29, 1429

addition to putting their troops in the Tourelles itself, the English also manned an earth and timber fortification built around the foot of that huge stone structure on its landward side, that is, on the south bank of the river. A short distance south of the Tourelles, the English converted a cluster of preexisting French buildings, known as the Augustins, into another fort. Five English forts formed an arc to the west, northwest, and north of Orléans. An additional fort stood on an island in the river to the west of the bridge, and still another fort was on the riverbank south of the fort on the island. The English fort known as Saint Loup stood on the north bank of the river, directly to the east of the city. Roughly opposite Saint Loup, on the south bank of the river, was the fort called Saint Jean le Blanc.

The critical weakness of the English deployment around Orléans was the huge gap between their forts northeast of the city. As long as this gap in the English chain of forts existed, the French could still, with great difficulty, get supplies and reinforcements into Orléans. French supply convoys had to cross from free France on the south bank of the Loire to the north bank at some considerable distance either up- or downstream from the city and the English forts. Once a French supply convoy was on the north bank of the river, it could thread its way through the English positions by way of the gap between the English forts northeast of the city. Then, the convoy could finally enter Orléans through the gate in the city's east wall. Obviously, this route was long, circuitous, and fraught with the danger of English interference. Nonetheless, this was precisely the route by which Joan, her army, and food supplies would enter the desperate city.

The English were far from unaware of the weakness in their position caused by the gap between their forts northeast of Orléans. Indeed, on the day of Joan's arrival, they had recently started construction on a new fort positioned to close this gap. It was at this point in their conduct of operations that the English had reason to bewail the sudden and rude departure of their Burgundian allies. It had been the intention of the English to employ the Burgundians as the garrison of the new fort that was intended to close the gap. The Burgundians quit the scene before the new fort could be completed.[11] Joan's arrival, and the train of events she set in motion, would ensure that the new fort would never be finished.

Joan, her army of about four thousand men, and a convoy of food supplies for the people of Orléans set out from the city of Blois on April 27, 1429.[12] Actually, at this point in the game, it is problematic to speak of Joan's army as being "her" army. She was under the escort of a clique of high-ranking French warrior nobles who still considered themselves to be the true leadership of the army. The French marched from Blois to Orléans along the south bank of the Loire. As an uneducated peasant, Joan was necessarily ignorant of the geographical details of any region she had not visited herself. She trusted the established official leaders of the army to bring her, by the proper route, to the direct confrontation with the English that she craved.[13] The army slept in the field on the night of April 27–28. Joan insisted on sleeping through the night wearing her armor.[14]

The army reached a point to the east of Orléans, on the south bank of the Loire, late on April 28. A hard, cold rain was pouring down, bringing a form of misery known to all veteran soldiers. It was at this point that the established leadership of the French army received their first taste of Joan's flaring temper. She had thought that she was being led directly to Orléans and the main part of the English army. She became livid when she realized that the city and the main forces of her enemies were on the other side of a broad river. She was convinced that the captains of the army had deceived her. Whether or not the established French military leadership really deliberately misled her cannot be proven either way with the evidence available today.[15]

Into the storm caused by Joan's temper came the Bastard of Orléans. He rode out of the east gate of his city, passed through the gap between the English forts to the northeast, turned south, and crossed to the south bank of the river. He was sincerely eager to meet Joan. It will be recalled that some weeks before, he had sent two emissaries to Chinon to make inquires about her. He knew that the people of his city were enthralled with Joan, even though they had not yet seen her. They had waited for her arrival with great impatience and greater hope.[16] Now, the Bastard was about to get his first initiation into the ways of the Maid.

During the series of battles that Joan participated in to break the English siege of Orléans, it was the Bastard who held the ultimate authority of command. Nonetheless, as was already becoming clear, Joan intended to be a loud and forceful voice in the conduct of operations.[17] The Bastard arrived in the French camp and presented himself to Joan, who stood in the rain with the captains of the rescue army. As he testified in Joan's posthumous retrial years later, the Bastard did not get a chance to properly introduce himself. Before he could even speak, Joan demanded, "Are you the Bastard of Orléans?" When the Bastard replied that he was and that he "rejoiced" at her arrival, she further demanded, "Was it you who counseled that I be brought to this side of the river and not directly against Talbot and the English?" (Lord John Talbot was the commander of the English forces besieging Orléans.) When the Bastard replied that he, and others wiser than himself, had decided to bring Joan to the side of the river away from the city and Talbot, she burst out, "In God's name, the counsel of God, my Lord, is surer and wiser than yours. You thought you had deceived me but it is you who have deceived yourselves, because I bring you better help than ever was given to a soldier or to a city, it is the help of the King of Heaven."[18] As was to become commonplace, Joan ascribed the source of her strategic and tactical insights to divine guidance. Whether she was sincere in this, or merely used the claim of divine guidance as a means to win the credibility that an illiterate peasant girl could never command on her own, is something that must forever remain unknown.

Joan was further irritated to learn that the captains of the army intended to turn the food convoy over to the Bastard and return with the army to Blois. Once at Blois, the captains planned to cross with the army to the north side of the Loire. They would then approach Orléans by marching north of the English forts, and, ultimately, they would pass through the gap in the English chain of forts northeast of the city. The Bastard, commendably keeping his composure, encouraged Joan to accompany him and the food convoy across the river and into Orléans. Joan was reluctant to part, even for a few days, from the army whose morals she had worked so hard to improve. She agreed to come with the Bastard and the food convoy into Orléans provided that Brother Pasquerel, her personal priest and confessor, returned with the army to Blois to ensure that there was no moral backsliding among the soldiers.[19]

The Bastard had already formulated a plan to get the food convoy from the south bank to the north bank of the Loire and thence into Orléans. He had arranged for a flotilla of boats to put out from Orléans and sail east up the river, past the English fort at Saint Loup, rendezvous with the food convoy on the south bank of the river east of the city, and then transport the food convoy across the river to the north bank. Once on the north bank, the food convoy would pass through the gap between the English forts northeast of Orléans and enter the city by the east gate. In order to make this trip eastward on the river, the boats would have to sail upstream, against the current. So, the boats needed a stiff wind blowing from west to east to fill their sails in order to overcome the current. The problem, as Joan, the Bastard, and the captains of the army stood in the rain on the south bank, was that the wind was blowing in precisely the wrong direction. Joan may have spoken some choice words about the situation that are not recorded by history. According to the accounts of the time, she merely said, "Wait a little, because, in God's name, all will enter the city." And then, at that very moment, the wind reversed direction. The Bastard and the captains must have gasped inwardly if they did not gasp outwardly. In any event, Joan's reputation as an envoy of the Almighty took an instant, upward leap.[20] The boats made their journey up the river, met Joan, the Bastard, and the food convoy on the south bank, and transported them to the north bank. (As per the Bastard's plan, the garrison of Orléans made a sortie to tie up the attention of the English in the fort at Saint Loup while the boats were passing by.[21]) As the army made ready to return to Blois on the south bank, Joan, the Bastard, and the food convoy billeted themselves for the night of April 28–29 in the village of Chécy on the north bank.[22]

At dusk on April 29, Joan, the Bastard, and the food convoy passed through the gap between the English forts northeast of Orléans and entered the city through the east gate. Remarkably, the English made no move to oppose them. As Joan passed through the gate and entered the streets of Orléans, there played out one of the great theatrical scenes of history. Throngs of people jammed the streets to give her a rapturous welcome, described in the chronicle known as the *Journal of the Siege of Orléans*. The *Journal,* written within a generation of Joan's death, reports that the people were "making such rejoicing as if they had seen God descend in their midst,.... And there was a marvelous press of people to touch her or the horse upon which she was."[23] Joan's inner state may well have been one of exultation as she felt the love of the masses sweep over her and as she realized that the consummation of her mission was at last at hand. Magnificent in her suit of armor, astride her white horse, she rode side by side with the Bastard through the joyous pandemonium. A member of her entourage carried her huge banner before her. There was a moment of horror as a corner of her smaller personal pennant accidentally caught fire from the torch of an overeager spectator. Swiftly and deftly maneuvering her horse, Joan snuffed out the flames with her own hands. There was a moment of stunned silence from the crowd, instantly followed by an outburst of acclaim for Joan's superb horsemanship. The happily riotous procession brought Joan clear across Orléans to the house where she would be staying at the west end of the city. The house belonged to the family of Jacques Boucher, treasurer of the city. Dismounting from her horse amid the tumult, she entered the house, took off her armor, ate a light supper, and went to sleep in the bed provided for her.[24]

Apparently, Joan spent most of the next day, April 30, engaged in intense discussion with the Bastard. It seems that he was feeling some anxiety as to whether the army would indeed return from Blois to Orléans via the north bank of the river. He announced to Joan his intention to journey to Blois personally to hold the captains of the army to their word.

Photo 6.1 Joan's entry into the streets of Orléans was one of the bona fide great theatrical scenes of history. As such, it has had an irresistible appeal to innumerable artists. The nineteenth-century painter J. J. Scherrer visualized it this way. © The Art Archive / Musèe des Beaux Arts Orléans.

Photo 6.2   This is the home of Jacques Boucher, treasurer of the city of Orléans, where Joan stayed during her time in the city. Actually, the original house was destroyed during World War II and subsequently rebuilt according to the original plans. © The Art Archive / Dagli Orti.

Meanwhile, the garrison of Orléans made an inconclusive foray toward the English fort that lay most directly north of the city. Joan took no part in this skirmish.[25]

Also on April 30, Joan sent her two heralds to deliver her letter of ultimatum to the English. Whether this letter was the same letter that Joan had dictated weeks before at Poitiers, or a new letter, cannot be ascertained with certainty from the evidence available today. Joan sent both her heralds on this mission, but only one returned, bearing the news that the English were holding the other herald prisoner. The English intended to burn the captive herald at the stake.[26] This was a gross violation of the universally understood laws of war. The persons of heralds were held to be sacrosanct. The action of the English against Joan's herald made brutally clear that they held her, and her entourage, to be outside the protections of the laws of war.

Angry at the English, but still eager to spare their lives if only they would be reasonable, Joan went out onto the Loire River bridge on the evening of April 30. She was protected from the English in the Tourelles by the barricade that the French had built across the bridge and by the gaps in the bridge where the English and French had broken the arches. Exercising her lungs, she shouted her ultimatum to the English who manned the mammoth stone towers that straddled the southern end of the bridge. The English replied by shouting obscene insults and threats to burn her if they ever caught her. Joan turned on her heel and went back into the city.[27]

The next day, Sunday, May 1, the Bastard departed for Blois by passing through the gap between the English forts northeast of Orléans. Joan, with a small contingent of soldiers and the swaggering French mercenary captain Étienne de Vignolles, better known as La Hire, escorted the Bastard between the English forts and then returned to the city. Most curiously, the English again failed to make any move to interfere with Joan and the Bastard. Joan spent most of the day riding her horse through the streets of Orléans, familiarizing herself with the city and receiving the cheers of the citizenry. Later, she again went out on the bridge and shouted her ultimatum at the English in the Tourelles; and again she was repaid for her concern with shouted obscenities.[28]

Joan spent May 2 riding her horse around the city to make a personal survey of the English positions, just as any responsible commander would.[29] She saw how the English did not have enough men to place them shoulder-to-shoulder all the way around Orléans. She also saw how they attempted to compensate for their inadequate numbers by grouping their men in the small forts that were scattered in a huge circle around the city. It would have been obvious to any intelligent person, Joan included as she rode around the city on her scouting mission, that she must strive to break the English encirclement as rapidly as possible—preferably by retaking the Tourelles to reopen the Loire River bridge and the direct route to free France.

On May 3, several small contingents of French troops from nearby towns made their way into Orléans through the incomplete English encirclement. Word came in that the Bastard, the main rescue army, and another large food convoy were on their way from Blois.[30]

The Bastard and his great column of men and supplies approached the gap between the English forts northeast of Orléans at dawn on May 4. Joan rode out from the city with 500 men to meet the Bastard and escort him and his column back into the city. Yet again, the English inexplicably failed to make any effort to interfere with a French force moving through the gap in their positions.[31] Was the presence of the Maid infecting the English with the same inertia that had previously afflicted the French?

The Bastard and his column entered Orléans with Joan and her force by the east gate and proceeded to get settled in. After lunch, the Bastard visited Joan at her lodging at the Bouchers' house. He informed her that a new and large English army, under the command of Sir John Fastolf, was rumored to be on its way from Paris to join the English already around Orléans. Apparently, Joan was cheerful to learn that yet more English were on their way to receive their rightful drubbing. Her squire, Jean d'Aulon, would testify years later at the retrial about what happened next. In one of her endearing transports of enthusiasm and hyperbole, Joan cried out, "Bastard! Bastard! In the name of God, I command you, that if you see the coming of Fastolf, and do not tell me about it, I will have your head cut off!" It is worth noting that Joan addressed the Bastard with the affectionate "tu" form of "you" instead of the formal "vous." The Bastard was probably amused by Joan's outburst. He replied, with some wit, that he had no doubt that she would do to him precisely what she threatened to do.[32]

After the Bastard took his leave, Joan and d'Aulon decided to lie down for a nap. As d'Aulon testified in the retrial, he was just dozing off when Joan bolted up from her bed and roughly rousted him from the couch where he was lying. When d'Aulon asked her what was the matter, she replied that her voices had just told her she must immediately ride against the English, though she did not yet understand if she was to attack the English forts around Orléans or Fastolf's approaching army. Within mere moments, Joan and d'Aulon could hear anguished cries going up from people in the street outside that the English were at that moment doing serious harm to the French. The Boucher household was in an instant state of bedlam as d'Aulon, along with Madame Boucher and her daughter Charlotte, helped Joan into her armor. Meanwhile, Joan's page, Louis de Coutes, according to his retrial testimony, scampered off to fetch her horse. Within minutes, Joan emerged from the Bouchers' house fully armed and mounted her horse. She told de Coutes to run into the house and find her banner, which he did. He handed Joan her banner through a second-story window and she took off at a gallop through the streets toward the east gate.[33] An eyewitness named Colette Milet stated in the retrial that the hooves of Joan's horse struck sparks from the pavement.[34] Approaching the east gate, Joan met wounded French fighting men streaming into the city. D'Aulon heard her say that the sight of French blood made her hair stand on end.[35]

Joan learned that the captains of the army had ordered an assault on the English fort of Saint Loup, east of the city. It was obvious to her that the assault was going badly. The fact that the captains launched the attack without informing Joan shows that they did not yet consider her part of the army's combat leadership. Joan spurred her horse out the east gate and across the fields to Saint Loup.

At the sight of Joan on her horse with her banner, at the sound of her voice shouting encouragement over the din, the French around Saint Loup rallied and went back on the attack with renewed ardor. They stormed up and over the walls of the fort and killed or captured every Englishman inside. A small force of English set out from their fort that lay directly north of Orléans with the intention of coming to the rescue of their comrades at Saint Loup. However, the English soldiers in this would-be rescue column scurried back to safety when they beheld a force of French coming to intercept them. Joan could rightfully claim her first victory in her first battle. Joan returned to the city among a swarm of French soldiers who were exultant over their first clear victory in years. But as Joan rode back over the field, she grieved equally for the French and English dead.[36]

Brother Pasquerel testified in the retrial that the next day, May 5, Joan refrained from fighting because it was the Feast of the Ascension.[37] The chronicler Jean Chartier claimed that also on May 5, the French military leadership in Orléans, headed by the Bastard, held a council of war without inviting Joan. They decided to launch a diversionary attack on the north side of the Loire River and a main attack on the south side. Still not trusting Joan to comprehend matters of strategy, they agreed that Joan would go with the diversionary attack but not be told of the main attack. Then they sent for Joan to tell her only as much of the plan as they wanted her to know. According to Chartier, Joan heard them out and then, intuitively figuring out that she was being used, went into one of her classic rages. "Tell me what you have really decided!" she shouted. "I know how to keep a bigger secret than that!" The Bastard pacified her by revealing the whole plan to her.[38] From that moment, it became standard procedure that Joan would always be at the forefront of whatever was the main attack on any given day of battle.

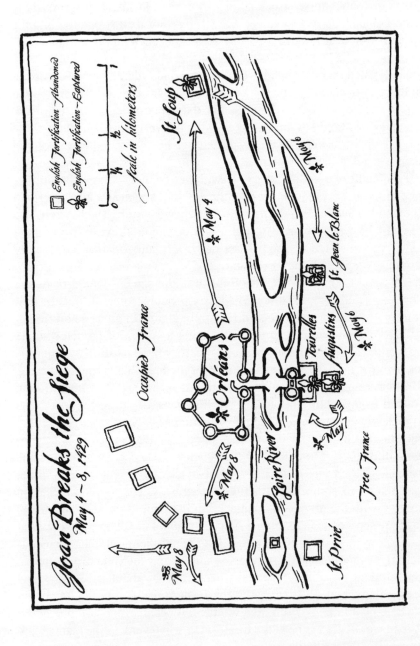

Map 6.2 Joan Breaks the Siege: May 4–8, 1429

Joan sent the English another written ultimatum on May 5, which Pasquerel quoted in his testimony for the retrial. She declared that "the King of Heaven warns and commands you through *me,* Joan the Maid, to abandon your fortresses and to return to your country, if not, I will make an uproar that will be remembered always" (emphasis mine).[39] Joan took this tone in many of the pieces of correspondence that she dictated to scribes and had sent to the powerful, both friends and enemies. Obviously, she had no doubts about the power of her own authority, even if, early in the game at Orléans, her friends and enemies were still trying to figure out what to make of her. Joan added a postscript to her letter offering to exchange some of the English prisoners from Saint Loup for her herald who was held captive by the English. Joan tied the letter to an arrow and told a crossbowman to shoot it into the English camp. As the man aimed his weapon and shot the arrow, Joan shouted to the English, "Read! Here is news!" The English did read, and when they finished reading, they replied with a chorus of shouts calling Joan a whore. This insult reduced Joan to tears until her voices spoke to comfort her.[40]

The next day, May 6, Joan and Captain La Hire had the leading parts in the French assault that took the English fort of the Augustins. The French forces used boats to cross from the north bank of the Loire to one of the many islands in the middle of the river. Marching across the island, they then reached the south bank via an improvised floating bridge built of boats. The French intended to attack the English fort at Saint Jean le Blanc. When the French got to the south bank, they were pleasantly surprised to discover that the English had abandoned Saint Jean le Blanc without a fight, withdrawing their men to the more distant fort at the Augustins. Satisfied with this situation, the French turned about to recross to the north bank of the Loire without having crossed swords with the English that day. Then, suddenly, the English came pouring out of the Augustins to attack the French from behind, hoping to turn the voluntary French withdrawal into an involuntary rout. As described in the previous chapter, it was only at this point that Joan and La Hire arrived on the scene. Joan and La Hire immediately leveled their lances and galloped their horses headlong at the English. This display of brazen courage by Joan and La Hire shamed the French soldiers into facing about en masse to join their two impetuous leaders in the attack. The French hustled the English back inside the fort of the Augustins. Then, in a frenzied and gory assault, the French stormed up and over the walls to hack down many English inside the Augustins and to chase the few survivors to safety in the Tourelles. The Tourelles was now the only important English fort left south of the Loire.

Some French troops spent the night in and around the newly liberated Augustins while other French troops, Joan among them, returned to Orléans via the temporary floating bridge and the boats. Joan was limping because, during the fight at the Augustins, she had stepped on one of the many small metal spikes (called "caltrops") that the English had strewn on the ground as a crude but effective precursor to modern landmines.[41]

That evening, according to Brother Pasquerel's retrial testimony, one of the captains came to visit Joan in her lodging at the home of the Bouchers. This man informed Joan that the captains had decided in council that they needed to wait for the arrival of more reinforcements from the Dauphin before making any more attacks on the English forts. Joan replied—icily, we may imagine—that "You have been with your council, and I have been with mine." That is, she had been receiving strategic guidance from her voices. "Believe," she continued, "that the counsel of my Lord will be accomplished and your counsel will perish." Turning to Brother Pasquerel, she instructed him to get out of bed the next morning earlier than he had previously. She predicted to him that she would have much to do, more than she ever had before, and that her blood would flow from above her breast.[42] That same night, the English abandoned their small fort, called Saint Privé, that stood on the south bank of the Loire to the west of the Tourelles.[43]

May 7 was Joan's great day of destiny. It was on this day that she played the decisive role in capturing the most important of the English forts that encircled Orléans: the Tourelles. Brother Pasquerel rose early, as Joan had instructed him to do the night before, and then performed a personal mass for her. As she was going out the door, she met a delegation of citizens of Orléans who entreated her to overrule the captains' decision to make no attack that day. Mounting her horse, Joan proclaimed, "In God's name, I will do it, and those who love me will follow me."[44]

Simon Charles, a high-ranking bureaucrat at the court of Charles VII, confirmed in his retrial testimony that the official French commanders in Orléans had decided against launching any attack that day. Joan achieved her ascendancy over the timid captains by forcing events to unfold *her* way. In his testimony, Simon Charles repeated the story that had been told to him by Raoul de Gaucourt, one of the highest-ranking warrior nobles serving France. De Gaucourt had positioned himself at the eastern gate of the city to prevent any French troops from going out to make an unauthorized attack. Then Joan showed up, in her armor, astride her horse, and with a throng of soldiers, both noble and common, behind her. Joan upbraided de Gaucourt as "a bad man" and angrily told him, "Whether you want it or not, the men-at-arms will go out, and they will win like they have won elsewhere." In the modern idiom, an armed peasant girl with the people behind her told a mighty noble of the realm to lead, follow, or get out of the way. Fearing for his life, de Gaucourt stood aside and Joan led the army out of the city.[45]

Joan and the army crossed to the south bank of the river once more via boats and the bridge of boats. D'Aulon testified that once she was outside the city, she summoned the French leadership *to come to her* for a war council.[46] The decision of this council was to attack the Tourelles immediately. Showing a confident and maniacal courage that they had not displayed for years, the French surged forward to place their scaling ladders against the walls, with Joan in the lead shouting encouragement. The English fought back with equally maniacal courage. It was during this attack that Joan famously took an English arrow through her shoulder—and, after the arrow was pulled out, returned to the fight to lead the final frenzied assault that stormed the Tourelles. With Joan and her banner in the lead, the exhausted but inspired French once more surged against the earth and timber fortification that was at the foot of the Tourelles.

While Joan and the army had been attacking the Tourelles from the south, the militia and people of Orléans took it upon themselves to join the fight. They improvised a portable wooden trestle to span the broken arches in the bridge, thereby enabling them to attack the Tourelles from the north side. Also, they took a boat, crammed it with combustible material, set it alight, and managed to wedge it under the wooden drawbridge that connected the main part of the Tourelles with the earth and timber fortification on the south bank of the river.[47]

The English in the earth and timber fortification, who were certain that Joan was dead, dissolved in panic as they beheld her storming at them again with the French army behind her. They tried to flee into the main, stone part of the Tourelles across the drawbridge that was now going up in flames from the incendiary boat wedged beneath it. It was at this moment that Joan memorably shouted at the English commander of the Tourelles, Sir William Glasdale, "Glasdale! Glasdale! Yield to the King of Heaven! You called me a whore, but I have great pity on your soul and the souls of your men!" When Glasdale tried to cross the burning drawbridge, it disintegrated beneath him. He, and several of his men, sank like stones to the bottom of the river in their heavy armor and drowned. Joan watched Glasdale meet his gruesome fate and then burst into tears with pity for his unshriven soul. The few English who were still left alive in the main stone part of the Tourelles quickly surrendered.[48] The Tourelles belonged to France once more.

Photo 6.3 Joan leads the attack on the Tourelles. This painting is a reasonably accurate depiction of the structure of the Tourelles and of the types of armor and weapons used in the battle. The painting does a more than adequate job capturing the frenzy of the struggle's climax. © Bettman/Corbis.

Years later, the Bastard testified in the retrial that he had wanted to break off the attack after Joan was wounded, but that Joan persuaded him to make one more supreme effort.[49] With the Tourelles back in French hands, the direct connection between Orléans and free France via the Loire River bridge was reopened. Joan returned in triumph to Orléans with an army that was truly on its way to becoming *her* army. She reentered the city to be greeted by the singing, shouting, and cheering of a populace demented with ecstasy. As church bells pealed out above the din, Joan gently and graciously forced her horse forward through the adoring mob. Reaching the Bouchers' house, she dismounted, went inside, had her armor removed, and received proper treatment for her wound. She ate a supper consisting of a few pieces of bread dipped in watered-down wine and finally collapsed in bed.[50]

The Bastard testified in Joan's retrial about what happened the next day. His recollection is amplified by the testimony of others and by the accounts in the *Journal of the Siege of Orléans* and in the *Chronicle of the Maid.*[51] The English abandoned their remaining forts around Orléans and drew up in battler order their now-reunified army to fight a climactic struggle in the open field. Joan and the Bastard led the French army out of the city and drew it up in battle order facing the English. Unable to bear the weight of her normal plate armor because of her wound, she wore a light shirt of chain mail. According to the accounts, Joan forbade the French from making an attack to initiate battle because it was Sunday, though of course she would allow them to defend themselves if attacked. The English also refrained from attacking. The two armies watched each other from opposite sides of the field for an hour without coming to blows. Eventually, the English turned about and marched away. The French let them go with some harassing pursuit by a small force under La Hire. The French discovered Joan's missing herald in one of the abandoned English forts. He was in shackles and rather the worse for wear, but he was alive.[52]

Edward A. Lucie-Smith, in his book *Joan of Arc,* rightly suggests that there was more than piety to the decision by Joan and the Bastard to forgo a final clash of arms at Orléans.[53] The English army in front of them was a unified whole that was no longer split up into small detachments in forts scattered around the city. The English were completely ready to meet a French attack. It is fair to assume that they were drawn up in their favorite formation with rows of longbowmen fronted with a barrier of sharpened stakes planted in the ground. This was the fighting technique with which the English had slaughtered French armies at Crécy, Agincourt, and other places over the years. The great weakness of this technique was that it was purely defensive in nature. The success of this standard English formation depended totally on the French being foolhardy enough to charge straight into it. For decades, the French had been precisely so foolhardy. But the Bastard was an intelligent man with recent and hideous memories of what it was like to charge such a position, and Joan was a fast and intuitive learner.[54] Between them, Joan and the Bastard would have none of it.

There were a few things that Joan, the Bastard, and the English all must have known. As the English stood in formation, hoping that the French would be foolish enough to attack them, everyone knew that the English supply line was a long and tenuous one that stretched back to Paris.[55] Everyone also knew that the French army could easily draw supplies from the city of Orléans, whose gates were immediately behind the French army. Moreover, the French had numerical superiority, with perhaps 6,000 Frenchmen facing about 4,000 Englishmen.[56] (The additional English force under Fastolf, that was supposedly on its way from Paris, had not appeared.) Because of their superior numbers, the French could have sections of their army take turns standing down to eat and rest, whereas the outnumbered English could do so only at much greater risk. Both sides knew that the English could win only if the French made a stupid frontal charge, but both sides also knew that, because of the supply situation, the French could stand there forever but the English could not. Any of these factors that Joan had not already perceived on her own could have been quickly and easily explained to her by the Bastard. Joan and the Bastard did what they needed to do to win. They waited. During the tense hour that the two armies stood glaring at each other, Joan ordered that an altar be brought out of the city and into the field and that two masses in a row be said for the French soldiers. Whether she did this out of piety, or because she was a master of psychological warfare, or both, is anyone's guess.

Regardless of what form her tactical reasoning took on the final day at Orléans, Joan "had done it." Orléans was saved. The myth of English invincibility was shattered. The fortunes of the Hundred Years' War would tip back and forth for years to come, but the decisive turning point was Joan's week of glory at Orléans.

Joan's primary contribution to the strategy employed by the French army at Orléans was to employ her overwhelming sense of urgency to browbeat her co-commanders into making the moves that were obviously correct but that they were too timid to make on their own. As we have seen, the first English fort that the French attacked after Joan's arrival at Orléans was Saint Loup. The fact that the French commanders launched the attack on Saint Loup without first informing Joan indicates that the

Bastard and his company retained for themselves the authority to make specific strategic decisions about which English forts to attack and in which sequence, at least at first. The Bastard and his cohorts apparently held the authority to decide to attack the fort at Saint Loup first, even if it took Joan's goading to get them to attack any English forts at all.

Saint Loup was the obvious candidate for the first attack on an English fort to break the English grip on Orléans. Firstly, it was the most isolated of all the English forts in its position on the north bank of the Loire to the east of the city. This meant that of all the English forts, the English would have the most difficulty sending a force of troops to reinforce or rescue its garrison if it came under overwhelming French attack. Secondly, the fort at Saint Loup was the most advanced point of the southern jaw of the English pincers that had almost, but not quite, completely encircled the city. It was the southern jaw of the English pincers—including the English forts at Saint Loup, Saint Jean le Blanc, the Augustins, and the Tourelles—that was most threatening to the city. This was because it was these forts of the southern jaw, particularly the Tourelles, that cut off Orléans from direct contact, reinforcement, and resupply from free France. As the most advanced point of the southern jaw of the English pincers, Saint Loup was the logical place for the French to begin their effort to pry the southern jaw open.

As we have seen, once the French captured Saint Loup, they continued to follow obvious strategic common sense by attacking and capturing Saint Jean le Blanc, the Augustins, and the Tourelles, in that sequence, in order to reopen the Loire River bridge and reestablish direct contact with free France. But as we have also seen, it took repeated harsh prodding from Joan to make the French commanders *act* on this obvious strategic common sense. Recall how she created pandemonium at the strategic planning meeting on May 5. Recall how she had to level her lance at the English to encourage her men to reverse their withdrawal and attack the Augustins on May 6. Recall how she overawed de Gaucourt when he tried to prevent any French troops from leaving Orléans on the morning of May 7. And finally, recall how, once she had humiliated de Gaucourt, she used her own authority to summon the French leadership to her side to make the momentous decision to storm the Tourelles immediately. By the morning of May 7, it just may have been that Joan had graduated from the role of merely goading her co-commanders to act speedily on their strategic common sense. In selecting the Tourelles as her target on May 7, she may have matured into the role of exercising strategic common sense for herself. Indeed, very early on the morning of May 7, even before her confrontation with de Gaucourt, she had announced to her hosts in Orléans, the Boucher family, that she would return to the city that evening by way of the main stone bridge over the river, a route that she could take only if the French were in possession of the Tourelles.[57]

JOAN'S TIME OF CONTINUED MILITARY SUCCESS

The defeatist French high command was almost as discomfited by Joan's sudden and astounding reversal of the course of the war as the English. In the days immediately following Joan's unexpected success, the Dauphin Charles dithered at the royal castle at Loches, holding interminable discussions with his civilian advisors about what to do next—and frittering away precious time as he did so. The Bastard came to Loches with Joan to urge immediate and aggressive action. He testified at Joan's retrial about what happened. Joan knocked on the door of the Dauphin's council chamber, entered, got on her knees before the Dauphin, and exhorted him to march on Reims with her to receive his crown. When one of the civilian advisors asked her about the source of her opinion, she went into a rapture describing how voices from God were urging her on.[58]

In his testimony, the Bastard went on to say that the military leadership of France favored reconquering Normandy before making the extremely risky thrust deep into Anglo-Burgundian territory to get to Reims. Joan countered by saying that it was essential to crown Charles as quickly as possible, because, once he was thus symbolically legitimized as the true king of France, "the power of his enemies would diminish continually until in the end they would be powerless."[59] We know from the testimony of Joan's cohorts that she was well informed about the dynastic and political realities of France and England.[60] Astute as she was, she must have understood the compelling reasons for Charles to be crowned quickly. Charles's mother, Isabeau of Bavaria, was known to have had extramarital liaisons, a fact she herself acknowledged. When Isabeau disinherited her son, the Dauphin Charles, by the Treaty of Troyes, giving the French crown to England's Henry, she let it be known that she doubted that her son the Dauphin was in fact the son of her husband, King Charles VI.[61] The Dauphin Charles's claim to be the rightful king of France as Charles VII was thus open to question by both his friends and enemies. Joan knew that if the Dauphin Charles could be properly anointed and crowned at Reims, as France's kings had been for centuries, the taint of his questionable parentage would vanish. She also knew that the act of anointing and crowning Charles in accordance with tradition would rally the people of

France to his cause as nothing else could. Conversely, this act would cast a fatal pall of doubt in the minds of French people on English pretensions to the French crown. In advocating an immediate march on Reims to crown Charles, Joan displayed an intuitive but sure grasp of how politics, public symbolism, and military action had to be integrated in formulating grand strategy. The Bastard affirmed in his testimony that the leadership embraced Joan's opinion.[62] An illiterate teenage peasant girl was now dominating the national policy decisions of France.[63]

Joan and the army set off for their next campaign. They would eliminate the remaining English forces along the Loire River and then drive on Reims with the Dauphin in tow. The English forces in question held fortified positions at the towns of Jargeau, Meung, and Beaugency. Each of these towns was either on, or very near, the banks of the Loire. This time, d'Alençon, not the Bastard, would hold the ultimate responsibility of command in the field. However, the *Journal of the Siege of Orléans* asserts that the Dauphin "placed the Maid in [d'Alençon's] company, expressly commanding him to behave and act entirely at her advice."[64] Regardless of how true this statement is, d'Alençon and Joan made a happy and brilliantly successful team. From June 12 to June 18, 1429, they stormed the fortified English positions at Jargeau and Meung, forced the surrender of the castle at Beaugency, and routed a large English army at the open-field Battle of Patay.[65]

Joan, d'Alençon, and their army marched into the suburbs of the English-held town of Jargeau on June 11—but only after aggressive Joan overruled her more cautious co-commanders, who were not eager to go on the offensive. Joan had about 8,000 men with her while the English in Jargeau numbered only about 700. It says something about the French commanders that even at those odds, it took a pep talk from Joan to get them to follow through on their plans to attack Jargeau. When the French entered the suburbs of the town, an English attack at first pushed them back. Then, as d'Alençon testified years later at Joan's retrial, the sight of Joan and her banner rallied the French soldiers. The French counterattacked and pushed the English back inside the fortress walls guarding the main part of town. That evening, in keeping with her character, Joan rode up to the walls and shouted her demand that the English surrender or suffer the consequences.[66] At Orléans, the English had answered Joan's shouted ultimatums with shouted obscenities and insults. At Jargeau, they answered with silence.[67] The next day, June 12, after a short preparatory bombardment by their gunpowder artillery, the French used scaling ladders to storm up and over the fortress walls of Jargeau. (*Again,* Joan had to

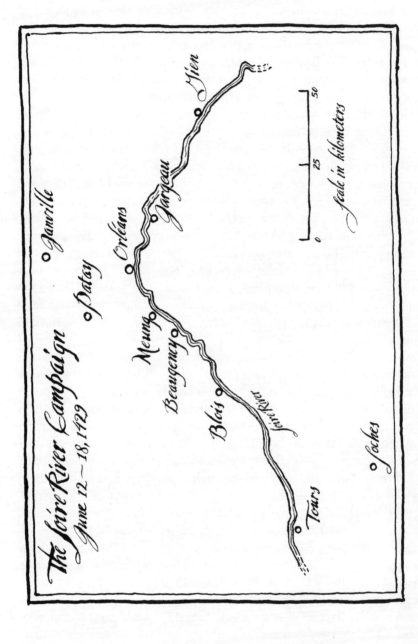

Map 6.3 The Loire River Campaign: June 12–18, 1429

give her co-commanders a verbal exhortation before they would agree to launch the final assault.) In a few swift hours, the French killed or captured all the English soldiers holding the town.[68]

D'Alençon testified that at Jargeau, Joan continued in her usual role of leading from out front, waving her banner and shouting encouragement to the soldiers. She was unfazed by a thrown stone that glanced off her helmet and knocked her to the ground as she was climbing up a scaling ladder. Instantly getting back on her feet, she shouted, "Friends, friends, up, up! Our Lord has condemned the English. At this hour they are ours. Have good courage!" According to d'Alençon, English resistance collapsed at that instant. D'Alençon also recalled that during the time the French were in the act of attacking the walls of Jargeau, Joan had warned him to step away from the spot where he was standing. Otherwise, Joan shouted, an English gunpowder weapon atop the walls, at which she was pointing, would kill him. D'Alençon did as Joan told him. To d'Alençon's astonishment, a short while later, a French soldier named du Lude was killed by the same gun that Joan had pointed to while he was standing exactly where d'Alençon had been standing. By his own testimony, d'Alençon gained renewed respect for Joan's prophetic gifts.[69]

After their liberation of Jargeau, Joan, d'Alençon, and the army moved against the English garrisons holding the fortified towns of Meung and Beaugency. On June 15, the French successfully stormed the English-held fortified stone bridge across the Loire River outside the town of Meung. Having seized the bridge, the French left part of their force to hold the bridge and to keep an eye on those English troops who still held the town of Meung, which lay some distance away. Joan, d'Alençon, and the main part of the army pushed on to Beaugency. Arriving at Beaugency, they quickly cleared the English from the town proper and surrounded the remaining English, who had taken refuge in the castle that stood near the middle of the town. The English in Beaugency castle surrendered on June 17, with the understanding that they would be allowed to march in safety toward English-held territory the next day. This they did.[70]

It was a good thing for the French that the English agreed to give up Beaugency on June 17. For, on that day, an English army of about 3,000 men appeared near Meung. This army, commanded by Lords John Fastolf and John Talbot, had just completed its march from English-controlled northern France, with the aim of rescuing the English forces at Jargeau, Meung, and Beaugency. (Fastolf had brought the army down from the north on his own. He had intended to go to Jargeau, but had given up on that plan when he realized the strength of Joan's army, which was, at that moment, attacking Jargeau. Later, Talbot had left Beaugency with a small force and joined Fastolf, even while the main English force in Beaugency was still holding out in the castle.) It was obvious to Fastolf and Talbot that they were dangerously late for a rescue mission.[71]

With the surrender of the English in Beaugency castle, the French escaped being pinned between the English in Beaugency castle and the English rescue army. Joan and d'Alençon marched their army from Beaugency toward Meung to meet the new English threat. On June 17, the French confronted the English rescue army as it stood drawn up in the classic English formation of longbowmen fronted with a hedge of stakes and supported by armored English knights on foot. However, using the same common sense that they had displayed on the last day at Orléans, the French refused to be drawn into making a foolish frontal assault on the English position—even when Fastolf tried to goad them on by issuing a formal challenge. The French refused to take the bait, and Fastolf felt his force to be too weak to attack the French. In another echo of the last day at Orléans, the English quit the field without any swords having been crossed or any arrows shot.[72]

The English fell back toward Meung. They intended to overpower the small French force that held the bridge at Meung, cross over the bridge to the south bank of the Loire, and then march to rescue the English force that they still believed to be holding Beaugency. After bombarding the French bridge position at Meung with their cannons through the night of June 17–18, the English learned of the surrender of their countrymen at Beaugency. At this news, the English rescue army finally gave up its mission as a failure and started to retreat toward sanctuary in northern France. The French took up the pursuit, Joan urging them on. It was now June 18, the day that would see the climactic and decisive French victory over the English in a battle fought in the open field near the town of Patay.[73]

At Patay, Joan was angry that the captains compelled her to march with the main body of the army instead of with the advance guard as was her habit.[74] La Hire commanded the advance guard, seconded by his longtime battle companion, Poton de Xaintrailles. La Hire pushed out for some distance a thin screen of horse-mounted scouts in front of the bulk of the advance guard. These scouts were to move surreptitiously forward through forests and fields to locate the English army and observe its numbers and disposition on the ground. Upon ascertaining this information about the English, the scouts were to send word back to La Hire while staying out of English sight. Near the town of Patay, the French scouts moved through a forest searching for the English. The English, who were marching northward as they retreated from the French, had received word from their own scouts that the French army was following them. The English halted to start readying a defense, but they still had no idea that the French were practically on top of them. As the French scouts picked their way forward through the trees, they suddenly heard the sportive English, whom they could not see, raise a shout of hunters' glee. A stag had bolted out of the trees and bounded among the English, who could not restrain their enthusiasm for the hunt and who sent up the happy hunters' shout that betrayed their position to the French. The English had no idea the French scouts were there. The French scouts then spotted the English establishing their defenses in a large clearing between some hedges. As per their orders, the scouts sent word back to La Hire.

La Hire came forward with the main force of the French advance guard. He discovered the still unaware English in the act of setting up their defensive position. The longbowmen were out of formation, driving in and sharpening their barrier of stakes. Seizing the moment, La Hire launched an immediate surprise attack with the advance guard. Bursting upon the stunned English, seemingly from out of nowhere, La Hire's swarm of horse-mounted knights trampled down the force of English that was nearest to them from one end of their position to the other. The French inflicted tremendous slaughter on this near group of English while a second, more distant English force fled the scene in panic. The English lost about 2,000 men out of a force of around 3,000, while French losses were practically nil.[75] In mere minutes, La Hire, with only the advance guard of the French army, inverted the result of Agincourt. Joan and the main body of the French army did not arrive on the battlefield until the fight was almost over.

In the aftermath of the Battle of Patay, the redoubtable Lord Talbot, England's foremost warrior leader after the death of King Henry V, found himself standing in front of Joan and d'Alençon as their prisoner of war. D'Alençon took advantage of the situation to tease Talbot by commenting that he, Talbot, had probably not thought that morning that he would become a prisoner of the French. Talbot could only reply by citing "the fortunes of war."[76] When the bedraggled and despairing Fastolf finally reached safety in English-held Paris, he had to endure the humiliation of being stripped of England's foremost award for service to the crown, the Order of the Garter, by the English regent in France, the duke of Bedford.[77]

To assess Joan's role as a military commander in the battles fought just after the siege of Orléans, it is necessary to examine her influence over both the strategy and the tactics of this part of the Hundred Years' War. "Strategy" is the conduct of war at the macro level. The strategist asks, "When and where, on a map of an entire country, do I want to force my enemy to meet me in a battle? How can I arrange several battles in sequence to win the war?" "Tactics" is the conduct of war at the micro level. The tactician asks, "I am about to meet my enemy in a battle on the specific piece of land in front of me; how can I arrange my different types of soldiers and weapons on this piece of land to win the battle?" In Joan's day, it was customary for the commander of an army to be deeply involved in questions of both strategy and tactics. (Modern armies and wars have become so huge that supreme commanders, such as Eisenhower in World War II, concern themselves only with strategy and the most general aspects of tactics. Subordinate commanders are now entrusted with tactical details.)

Trying to gauge Joan's influence over the tactics of the battles fought at Jargeau, Meung, Beaugency, and Patay is problematic. The record contained in the original documents of the time is thin on this question. Certainly Joan exercised complete control over the *type* of tactics employed by her army. At Jargeau, for example, she could have chosen the tactic of surrounding this English-held walled town and then subjecting it to a siege of many days or weeks to starve out the defenders. Instead, she opted for the tactic of direct assault—where the direct assault was characterized by using scaling ladders, inspirational leadership, and pure guts to storm up and over the walls to seize an enemy position in a single day. While Joan clearly chose the type of tactic she wanted her army to employ at Jargeau, it is difficult to judge if she was involved in the tactical details of arranging her soldiers on the ground to carry out her preferred tactic. (But then, d'Alençon's general comment in his retrial testimony—that Joan "excelled" at "placing the artillery"[78]—*does* give us a tantalizing suggestion that she got down into the tactical minutiae of placing each big gun for the bombardment at Jargeau.)

Though one recent author, Lieutenant-Colonel de Lancesseur, has tried, there is no way to measure to what extent, if any, Joan influenced the tactical details of arraying the troops at the Battle of Patay. De Lancesseur claims in his book *Jeanne d'Arc, Chef de Guerre,* that at Patay, Joan invented the tactic of using gunpowder artillery to make a preparatory bombardment on enemy defenses in a battle fought in the field (as opposed to in a static siege). This scarcely seems credible. De Lancesseur cites no supporting source documents and there is neither eyewitness testimony from Joan's retrial nor any wording in the major chronicles that back his claim. Contemporary French scholar Michel de Lombarès, in his article on Patay, paints a picture that aligns much better with the original source documents. He describes the battle as a quick, one-sided massacre in which La

JOAN'S ACHIEVEMENT AS A MILITARY COMMANDER 73

Hire achieved total surprise on the unprepared English. La Hire was able to launch an immediate charge from an unexpected direction at an unexpected time—a charge that trampled many English and scattered the rest before Joan could do anything herself to influence the tactical situation.[79]

While Joan's influence on tactics in the battles fought shortly after the siege of Orléans is an open question, her influence on overarching strategy was clearly paramount. Perceval de Cagny, d'Alençon's personal chronicler and a witness to many of these events, recorded that on June 14, Joan called d'Alençon to her side. She then *told* him, "Tomorrow after dinner I want to go see Meung. Have the company ready to leave at that hour."[80] D'Alençon did as he was told, and cheerfully, so far as can be determined. Joan's decision to attack the English at Meung at a time of her choosing was a decision in the realm of strategy. The fact that the French used the tactic of an immediate assault, rather than a deliberate siege, to take the English-held bridge at Meung again shows Joan's influence. But as at Jargeau, it is impossible to delineate precisely how much she influenced the tactical details of arranging the French troops on the ground at Meung.

Joan's order to d'Alençon to move against the English troops at Meung from her base of operations in Orléans suggests that she was anticipating a strategic gambit used repeatedly by Napoleon: the "strategy of the central position."[81] After Joan's conference with Charles at Loches, she, d'Alençon, and their army had set up their base of operations in the recently liberated city of Orléans. Nineteen kilometers to the east, on the Loire River, an English garrison held the walled town of Jargeau. In the opposite direction, twenty-one kilometers west from Orléans, another English force held the fortifications at Meung. Eight kilometers farther to the west from Meung, a third English contingent held the castle and town walls at Beaugency. By establishing her sizable army at Orléans, in the "central position" *between* these widely scattered English garrisons, Joan prevented her foes from uniting into a single force big enough to be a threat. Trusting the small garrison in Orléans to keep an eye to the west, Joan first made a high-speed strike to the east with her entire field army to storm Jargeau. Doubling back on her steps with the same high speed, she returned to Orléans and then struck west to overwhelm Meung and Beaugency before the English in those two towns could coordinate an effective defense. The final touch of perfection on these maneuvers was that Joan completed them *before* the large English army coming down from the north could intervene to rescue the scattered English detachments at Jargeau, Meung, and Beaugency. As previously related, the English rescue army did arrive on the scene at Meung, but too late to achieve anything. This English army was the same army that Joan and her cohorts caught and destroyed at Patay as it vainly tried to escape back to the north.

During the fighting at Meung and Beaugency, but shortly before the battle at Patay, circumstances led Joan to make a crucial policy decision on her own authority that affected all France. It is necessary to digress to explain a knotty political situation. The great Breton nobleman, Arthur de Richemont, held the title "Constable of France," making him, in theory, the supreme commander of France's armies in the field. In 1428, a year before Joan first presented herself to the Dauphin Charles, de Richemont had fallen victim to the intrigues at Charles's court. He suffered a falling-out with Charles's favorite advisor, the obese Georges de La Trémoïlle. Charles sided with La Trémoïlle, exiling de Richemont from court. De Richemont returned to his lands in Brittany to wait for a better moment.[82] (Two years after Joan's death, La Trémoïlle's enemies at court tried to assassinate him. His life was saved by the fact that his assailants' daggers cut only fat.[83])

While Joan, d'Alençon, and their troops were engaging the enemy at Meung and Beaugency, de Richemont suddenly appeared on the scene with his sizable personal army behind him. He demanded that he be allowed to join in the war against the English. Charles had already expressly forbidden Joan and d'Alençon to have anything to do with de Richemont. By his own testimony at the retrial, d'Alençon was ready to obey the Dauphin's orders.[84] Joan was suddenly faced with the real possibility that de Richemont and d'Alençon would start yet another French civil war, even while English troops were still present at Meung and Beaugency and while a large English army was known to be on its way to rescue the English in those two towns. The modern mind boggles at the tangles of feudalism. De Richemont was willing to make war *against* the Dauphin in order to win the right to make war *for* the Dauphin—and d'Alençon was willing to take him up on the issue.

D'Alençon testified at the retrial about how Joan intervened to resolve the situation in a sane fashion, disobeying the Dauphin's orders as she did so. She told d'Alençon that it was "necessary to help each other." She then stood face-to-face with de Richemont and told him, "Ah! Handsome Constable, you are not come because of me, but since you are come, you are welcome." By her willingness to defy Charles's orders with a snap decision of her own, Joan averted a catastrophe—and added a formidable warrior leader and his men to her army.[85]

After bringing de Richemont and his force into her army, Joan employed them against the English at Beaugency. When the English at Beaugency surrendered, Joan next had to turn her attention to the impending crisis of the Battle of Patay. Her co-commanders, as usual, went into a dither about what to do. As usual, they consulted her, and as usual she carried them along with her advice to take the most aggressive course and seek battle. Also as usual, she expressed her opinion in rhetorical flights. D'Alençon testified that she cried out, "In God's name, we must fight them! If they were hanging from the clouds we would have them, for God has sent them to us for us to punish them."[86] The Bastard recalled that she loudly said, "Do you all have good spurs?" When she was asked if this meant that they should retreat, she hotly replied no, they would need good spurs to chase after a fleeing enemy.[87] Their spines thus stiffened, the French went on to win their greatest victory to that point in the war.

The record seems clear that even if Joan's co-commanders handled the tactical details at Jargeau, Meung, Beaugency, and Patay, it was Joan herself who drove the overarching strategy of *forcing* a battle to take place at each of those locations. Joan's decision to accept de Richemont and his men into her army, against the orders of the Dauphin, was likewise a strategic decision of the highest order. The overall French conduct of military operations in June 1429 seems to indicate that Joan was truly a master strategist.

After the decisive triumph at Patay, it was time to get Charles to Reims.[88] Joan had to contend with yet more procrastination by the Dauphin. Finally losing her patience, she left the royal court and camped out with the army for two days and nights in the fields near the town of Gien. This act stirred Charles from his lethargy and indecision.[89] On June 30, Joan and her co-commanders set out for Reims at the head of the army, now swollen to 12,000 men.[90] The Dauphin Charles came along, a prisoner of the success of his own subjects.

The crisis of the march on Reims came when the city of Troyes closed its gates in the faces of Joan, the Dauphin, and the army. Troyes became the apogee of Joan's career as a true battle commander. Troyes was strongly defended and the supply situation of the army was tenuous. After several days of vacillation by Charles, Joan once more had to impose her will on a royal war council by demanding immediate, aggressive action. "In God's name, within three days I will make you enter that city by love or by strength and force" was how the Bastard recalled her exhortation to battle. "Then," he continued,

> the Maid advanced immediately with the royal army, pitched the tents along the ditches, and took such admirable precautions as would not be taken by the two or three most experienced and famous chiefs of war. She

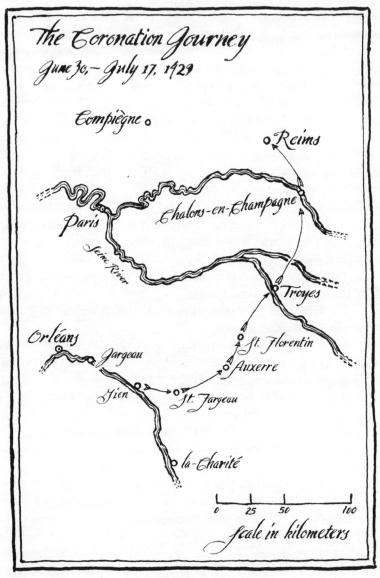

Map 6.4 The Coronation Journey: June 30–July 17, 1429

worked so much that night that the next day the bishop and citizens of the city, afraid and trembling, placed themselves in royal obeisance.[91]

Jean Chartier claimed in his chronicle that Joan took charge of placing the big cannons to aim them at the walls.[92] Simon Charles, that observant royal court bureaucrat, was present at these events. He testified that it was

Joan who gave the orders to make bundles of tree branches with which to fill in the moat and Joan who gave the order to commence the attack—and then the city surrendered in terror without a fight.[93] This is the clearest case we have to show that a teenage peasant girl was the true commander of the royal army of France.

In the aftermath of the surrender of Troyes, Joan again revealed how highhanded she could be when her sense of what was morally right demanded it. By the terms of the surrender of the city, the English garrison was allowed to march out and head to safe territory with its horses, armor, weapons, and other property. Part of its "property" consisted of a number of French prisoners who had yet to be ransomed. When Joan saw these men trudging out through the gate of Troyes guarded by their English captors, she went into one of her magisterial displays of righteous indignation. Flouting the protocols of chivalry regarding the ransoming of prisoners, she demanded the immediate release of her countrymen. Tense moments followed until Charles intervened to pay the prisoners' ransoms on the spot, desperate though his financial situation already was.[94]

The march to Reims continued. On July 17, 1429, beneath the soaring vaulted ceiling of Reims cathedral, Charles felt the crown come to rest on his head while the warrior girl who put it there stood beside him, magnificent in her shining armor.

JOAN'S TIME OF DIFFICULTY

Shortly before the coronation, Joan had sent a letter to Philip, the duke of Burgundy, urging him to make peace with Charles and inviting him to attend the coronation. Philip had declined. The same day as the coronation, Joan dictated a second letter to Philip. She respectfully but forcefully admonished him, "by God in heaven," to break off his alliance with the English and to return to his proper place of fealty to the newly crowned King of France. She told Philip that if he and Charles still wanted to make war, they should join forces and "go against the Saracens" on a new crusade to free the Holy Land from the infidels.[95] Philip's reply was cold silence.

The day Charles received the crown, he started to knock the legs out from underneath the people whose courage had brought him to the crown.[96] The moment was perfect for an immediate march on Paris to take back France's capital. The English and Burgundians were in panicked disarray and the city was weakly defended. Instead, the timid and easily duped Charles immobilized the army and Joan while he entered into nego-

Photo 6.4 This statue in the great cathedral at Reims depicts Joan as she may have looked during Charles's coronation. A replica of her banner is displayed behind the statue. © The Art Archive / Dagli Orti.

tiations with the enemies of his people and his country. Weeks dragged by while the English and Burgundians used the negotiations as a cover to massively reinforce the garrison of Paris and to refurbish the city walls. Joan and d'Alençon could only seethe in fury.

Joan stood by in growing dismay as Charles and his circle of civilian advisors froze her out of high-level decision making, starting the instant Charles had the crown safely on his head. On August 5, she attempted to regain control of events. She dictated a public letter to the people of Reims that is astounding for what it reveals of a former farm girl trying to make strategic policy against the will of her king:

> My dear and good friends the good and loyal Frenchmen of the city of Reims, Joan the Maid sends you her news, and begs and requires you to have no doubt about the good fight she is waging for the blood royal; and I promise you and certify that I will never abandon you as long as I live. And it is true that the king has made a truce with the duke of Burgundy lasting fifteen days, by which he [the duke of Burgundy] will surrender the city of Paris to him peacefully at the end of those fifteen days. Nevertheless, you should not marvel at seeing me not enter that city so swiftly, no matter how many truces are made, I am never content and do not know if I will keep them; but if I do, it will only be to preserve the honor of the king; no matter how much they mock the blood royal, I will hold the army of the king and keep it together lest, at the end of those fifteen days, they do not make peace. For that, my very dear and perfect friends, I beg you not to make yourselves uneasy about this as long as I live; I require that you keep good watch and guard the good city of the king; and let me know if there are any traitors who would do you grief, and briefly, I will do all I can to combat them; and let me know your news. I commend you to God who will guard you.
>
> Written on Friday, the fifth day of August, from a camp in the fields on the road to Paris.[97]

Joan's ultimatums to the English at Orléans, her rapprochement with Arthur de Richemont before the Battle of Patay, her two letters to the duke of Burgundy, and her letter to the people of Reims all exemplified a specific trait of hers. This trait was her amazing habit of arrogating to herself, *a peasant girl,* the authority to treat with high-ranking paladins and heads of state as equals as she tried to shape the policy of a kingdom to suit her own vision of how things must be. From April to July 1429, she made this supreme audacity work. Starting in July 1429, it all fell apart for her.

On August 15, Joan and d'Alençon led the French in an inconclusive confrontation with a large Anglo-Burgundian army at Montépilloy. At Montépilloy, the French again refused to commit themselves to an attack on a prepared and ready English defensive position. After some sharp but indecisive skirmishing, the opposing armies parted and marched away. (In the course of the skirmishing, Charles's favorite advisor, the hugely obese Georges de La Trémoïlle, fell off his horse. In what must have been a grimly comic scene, the members of La Trémoïlle's entourage had to struggle to hoist him back into the saddle.)[98]

After several more days, it became clear that the duke of Burgundy had reneged on his promise to surrender Paris to Charles. At last, on September 8, weeks after the ideal moment to strike had passed, Charles allowed his champions to attack the city walls. Joan suffered her first repulse, made even more bitter by an arrow shot through her thigh. The arrow struck her while she was testing the depth of the moat with her lance and shouting threats at the Burgundian soldiers on the walls above her. Another arrow killed one of her pages, an adolescent boy named Raymond, while he was carrying her banner. For some time after she was wounded, Joan stuck to her position at the edge of the moat, shouting encouragement to her men. Eventually, and over her loud verbal protests, a group of high-ranking French nobles bodily picked her up and carried her out of the battle. With that act, the French broke off their attacks for the day. One of the nobles who forcibly took Joan out of the fight was Raoul de Gaucourt, the man she had overawed and humiliated when he had tried to prevent her from leaving the city of Orléans on her way to attack the Tourelles.[99]

Now, Charles's conduct veered close to treason. The day after Joan was wounded, she and d'Alençon intended to renew the attack on Paris. Instead, Charles summoned the two of them into his presence for a conference to consider the question of what to do next. This conference took up all of September 9. On September 10, Joan and d'Alençon set out with their troops to attack Paris from a different direction by crossing the Seine River over a timber bridge, which d'Alençon had ordered built for just that purpose. Their rage and disgust had to be total when they discovered that the bridge had been secretly demolished on *Charles's* orders. Charles ordered a retreat back to the territory that had always been his. On September 21, he disbanded the great army with which Joan, the Bastard, d'Alençon, and the rest had saved France. Joan and her loving circle of co-commanders went their separate ways, never to see each other again.

Charles made the heartbroken warrior girl a virtual prisoner of his royal court, though he ensured that she was honored and fêted. When d'Alençon wrote to Charles asking that he send her to help him fight to recover his lands in Normandy, Charles and his civilian advisors refused. Charles's favorite advisor, diplomat Georges de La Trémoïlle, hated Joan for the way her leadership of the army had aborted his policy of negotiation with Burgundy. He also surely hated her for the way she had joined forces with his personal rival, Arthur de Richemont, just before the Battle of Patay. There is no doubt that La Trémoïlle was the main force conspiring at court to frustrate Joan's and d'Alençon's plans following Charles's coronation in Reims.[100]

Unfortunately for historians, the eyewitness accounts of Joan's military activities thin out considerably for the period following the disbandment of her great army. The Bastard and d'Alençon were the two most important witnesses in Joan's posthumous retrial with regard to her martial prowess. After Charles disbanded the army and sent these two men on their way, they never saw her again. Historians are thus deprived of any commentary from Joan's two closest warrior comrades concerning her later military career. Still, there is a happy side to this situation. The testimonies of the Bastard and d'Alençon about Joan's words and deeds from Orléans to Paris, combined with the testimonies of others and the record of the chronicles, are enough to establish for modern scholars the essential qualities of Joan's military leadership.

After Charles disbanded the main French army, Joan continued to carry on the war as an independent captain, leading such meager troops as the king allowed her, plus what she could raise on her own. A significant percentage of her force consisted of non-French mercenaries. Her influence on grand strategy had sunk to nil, but her tactical autonomy increased.[101] For example, Charles and his advisors told her that her new strategic objective was to take the Burgundian towns of Saint-Pierre-le-Moûtier and La Charité on the upper Loire River. Once Joan arrived outside Saint-Pierre-le-Moûtier with her little army in October 1429, however, she had the final word on the local tactical operations aimed at actually seizing the town. In November, she led her troops in another of her trademark direct assaults that carried her men up and over the enemy's walls to win the day. Once inside the town, she had to exert her moral authority to the utmost to stop her band of mercenaries from plundering the church.[102]

Joan next moved against the town of La Charité. She continued to manifest the skills of a true military commander. For example, just before she laid siege to La Charité, she dictated a letter to the citizens of the town of Riom that contained thoroughly practical requests for various kinds of supplies. The authentic original letter is still held in the archive in Riom.[103] But the old magic was gone for Joan. Her largely mercenary force could not give her the same loving loyalty that her great army, drawn from the best of all France, once had. Her siege of La Charité failed, mostly for lack of logistical support from Charles, but also because her jaded mercenaries lacked the spirit to respond to her style of leadership. For these non-French mercenaries, one of the primary motivations for fighting was the hope for plunder. As they had just found out at Saint-Pierre-le-Moûtier, their saintly commander would not allow them to plunder, thereby diminishing their willingness to follow her into danger. Joan had to withdraw her army from around La Charité and return to her place at the royal court. Charles's conferring titles of nobility on her and her family in December did little to make her feel better.[104]

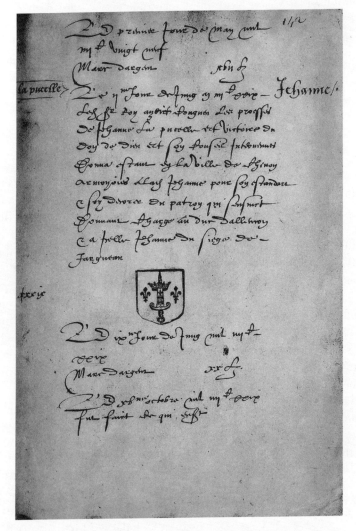

Photo 6.5   Charles conferred titles of nobility on Joan and her family with this official document around Christmastime in 1429. "Jehanne La Pucelle" is fifteenth-century French for "Joan the Maiden." The document includes a sketch of Joan's new coat of arms: an upward-pointing sword supports the crown of France, flanked by two fleurs-de-lis. Only members of the top tier of French nobility were allowed to include the fleur-de-lis in their coats of arms, so the honor conferred on Joan was high indeed. © The Art Archive / Joan of Arc birthplace Domrémy France / Dagli Orti.

An episode from this later, grimmer phase of Joan's military career demonstrates that for all her reputed saintliness, she had a tough-minded appreciation for the uses of power. On a day in April 1430—the precise date is unknown—she led her small personal army, augmented by some local troops, in annihilating a Burgundian contingent in a battle in the open field near the town of Lagny. She took as prisoner the leader of the enemy force, a local freebooting warlord named Franquet d'Arras. D'Arras had earned the hatred of the communities in the area by his atrocities and depredations. Before the battle at Lagny, Joan had learned that one of the leaders of a failed anti-English revolt in Paris was being held prisoner by the English. After taking d'Arras prisoner, Joan attempted to exchange him for her fellow French patriot held captive in Paris. Then she learned that the man whose freedom she wanted to obtain using d'Arras as a bargaining pawn had already been executed. With d'Arras no longer of any use to her, she handed him over to the local authorities with the cold-sounding words, "Since my man is dead, whom I wanted, do with this one that which is required by justice." After a two-week trial, d'Arras was convicted of murder, robbery, and treason and put to death. Joan was criticized by both her friends and enemies for her treatment of d'Arras. As a prisoner with at least some noble blood in him, the rules of chivalry dictated that he should be returned to his own people after they paid a suitable ransom for him. The farm girl whose tender heart had made her weep over enemy dead on several battlefields seems to have grown some calluses on her soul—or perhaps her original peasant sense of what constituted justice won out over her acquired aristocratic sensibilities.[105]

The Battle of Lagny was Joan's last victory. She had only a month of freedom left in her life until a swarm of Burgundians yanked her out of her saddle in a melee fought beneath the city walls of Compiègne. Ahead of her lay the ever-darkening road to captivity, torment, and martyrdom.

JOAN'S CAREER AS A COMMANDER: AFTERMATH AND ASSESSMENT

Joan died screaming Jesus' name as the flames engulfed her in the central square of Rouen on May 30, 1431. The Hundred Years' War would go on without Joan, its fortunes swaying back and forth, for another twenty-two years; but the cause for which she died would triumph. Her career as a soldier was an absolutely essential element of that triumph. She found the cause of France in its death throes, she brought that cause back to robust life, and she put that cause on the long and difficult climb to eventual victory.[106]

In the years immediately after Joan's death, desultory fighting continued, with the English getting slightly the better of numerous minor battles and sieges.[107] The French fighting men seem to have retained only part of the spark Joan had given them. Joan's old stalwart La Hire became a prisoner of the English for a brief time. King Charles's ability to make war on his English and Burgundian enemies was hampered by a simple lack of cash with which to maintain an army in the field. He no longer had Joan there to inspire men to serve without pay and with only the most meager rations.

Another of the Hundred Years' War's several key turning points came in 1435. Philip, duke of Burgundy, renounced his alliance with England and allied himself to his former enemy, Charles VII of France, by the Treaty of Arras. This treaty was a catastrophe for English ambitions in France. With their small population and resource base, the English could only hope to dominate France by exploiting the civil war between the Burgundian French and the free French who supported the Valois dynasty of Charles. The Treaty of Arras ended the French civil war upon which English success depended. England was now at war with the combined forces of Burgundian and Valois France. Paris was a Burgundian holding with a small English garrison. In 1436, that English garrison left town and the forces of a now reunited kingdom of France marched in to take possession of their capital.

The English stubbornly fought on against apparently impossible odds, and, for a while, it looked as if they might actually succeed. From 1436 to 1440, various small English contingents successfully defended Calais against a Flemish-Burgundian siege, routed a much larger French force at Ry, seized Pontoise by trickery, broke up Burgundian and French attempts to besiege Le Crotoy and Avranches, and, finally, retook Harfleur for England. It seemed as if the English reputation for martial brilliance and the French reputation for martial bumbling were firmly back in place. In 1441, the French recovered a portion of their pride. King Charles VII of France, in a new departure, finally deigned to accompany his own army into the field without having to be dragged by a headstrong girl in armor. He led his force in a siege to retake Pontoise from its English garrison. Dazzling maneuvers by an English relief column forced the French to temporarily break off the siege. But Charles, growing the first backbone of his life, persisted and eventually took Pontoise.

Back in England, a war-weary peace faction took control of the government and, in 1444, negotiated a truce with Charles that would last for five years. Charles and his top military advisors put those five years to superb use. They scrapped the antiquated, feudal-style French army with its

JOAN'S ACHIEVEMENT AS A MILITARY COMMANDER 85

hodgepodge of foolishly individualistic nobles and their retinues, wretched peasant levies, and unreliable mercenaries. This was the outmoded feudal army that had incurred disaster after disaster and that only Joan had been able to lead to repeated victories. To create a new French army, Charles decreed the raising of the *compagnies d'ordonnance*. With these new forces, France acquired the first professional, permanent, national standing army that Europe had seen since Rome. As a decisive bonus, the technocratic Bureau brothers, Jean and Gaspard, gave this army a state-of-the-art gunpowder artillery force that was without peer.[108] It should be noted that the reforms of the French army owed nothing to Joan. She was one of the last leaders of the old French army, not one of the first leaders of the new French army.

When fighting resumed in 1449, the new French army smashed everything English in its path. The Bureau brothers' cannons quickly pulverized one English-held fortress town after another. In two desperately hard-fought battles, at Formigny in 1450 and at Castillon in 1453, the French annihilated two English armies in succession. English power in France evaporated. The French generously allowed the English to retain a tiny enclave around Calais and the Hundred Years' War came to its end. France had taken its first steps toward becoming a modern nation-state. Two of Joan's old comrades, Arthur de Richemont and the Bastard (now bearing the title "count of Dunois"), were leaders in the new French army that completed her work.[109] No doubt they thought of her on the day of final victory.

It is clear that the military fortunes of the free Valois French for whom Joan had fought suffered ups and downs after she left the scene. But it is also clear that if Joan had not done what she did when she did it, Valois France would *never have survived* to experience those subsequent ups and downs on the way to eventual victory. A number of factors—Joan's career, the defection of the Burgundians from the English, the limited resource base of England, and the reforms of the French army—were each and all necessary for France to win in the end. Joan's career was one of several essential factors, but an essential factor it was.

The cumulative testimony of her comrades in arms shows that Joan was no mere inspirational figurehead. She was repeatedly present when key decisions were being made in councils of war, and she repeatedly forced those decisions to reflect her expressed will. To what extent her strategic and tactical opinions were the product of her own rational military calculations or of her belief in otherworldly inspiration can never be known. Still, one may attempt to draw the organizational chart of the French high command however one chooses, but the fact is that *Joan was the ultimate driving power behind every aggressive move the French army made.*

Given that so much of our understanding of Joan is based on the testimony given at her posthumous retrial, it is necessary to address the question of just how truthful the testimony was. Charles VII had a vested interest in the Church clearing the name of the girl to whom, in the prevailing view, he owed his crown. This suggests that there would have been pressure on those testifying at Joan's retrial to remember her in a favorable light. However, it was probably beyond the means of even a king to forcibly yet covertly orchestrate the testimony of 115 witnesses representing all social classes who were questioned over a period of several years in widely separated regions of France.

There is just enough variation in overlapping pieces of testimony to show that, while the people testifying saw the same events, they were not reciting a contrived scenario that had been forced on them. For example, the Bastard and Brother Pasquerel, who was Joan's personal priest and confessor, were both eyewitnesses to French efforts to transport supplies to Orléans by boats on the Loire River the day Joan arrived outside the city. Testifying at the retrial years after the event, the Bastard recalled that the resupply mission succeeded because a sudden change in the way the wind was blowing enabled the boats to travel in the needed direction. Brother Pasquerel, by contrast, testified about a sudden rise of the water level of the river that enabled the boats to proceed.[110] For another example, the Bastard, Brother Pasquerel, Jean d'Aulon (Joan's squire), and Louis de Coutes (her page) all gave eyewitness testimony in the retrial about the fight at the Tourelles. These men agreed on the key points: Joan was wounded by an English arrow, and, notwithstanding her wound, she was the driving force behind the attack. However, each of these men provided numerous additional details in his testimony that the other three did not. These variations in detail include Brother Pasquerel's description of the treatment of Joan's wound, the Bastard's description of how she went off alone to pray, d'Aulon's description of how she had to wrestle her banner from a momentarily confused friendly soldier, and so forth.[111] The variations in the retrial testimony of Joan's close companions demonstrate that they were *not* coached or coerced into glorifying her for Charles's political benefit.

D'Alençon and the Bastard were the two most important witnesses as far as establishing Joan's role as a military leader was concerned. Significantly, d'Alençon detested Charles and was in fact involved in a failed plot against him some years after Joan died. D'Alençon would be arrested for treason less than a month after he gave his testimony about Joan. Sadly, d'Alençon and the Bastard would be on opposite sides of this failed conspiracy. It would be the Bastard who would arrest d'Alençon on Charles's orders.[112] D'Alençon's hatred for Charles meant that he was hardly in a mood to cooperate with Charles by saying good things about Joan just to enhance Charles's legitimacy as king. D'Alençon must have been motivated to praise Joan's skills as a military leader by a sincere sense of admiration for his long-dead friend.

Finally, it is a standard characteristic of the warrior nobility of any culture to possess a large measure of egotism. The Bastard, d'Alençon, and all the rest would not have been exceptions to this rule. Why would men such as that have made up stories that exaggerated the role of a teenage peasant *girl* telling them what to do? The very improbability of them saying what they did leads one to conclude that they were saying things that were remarkable but true.

Chapter 7

JOAN'S LEADERSHIP QUALITIES: THE FIRST PART OF "HOW"

JOAN'S APPARENT SKILLS OF COMMAND

Making herself the icon of inspiration for the army and the people and, in her own way, commanding the army in war—this is *what* Joan did. But *how* did she do it? What was it about her that enabled her to do what she did?

First of all, Joan had to possess an innate genius that enabled her, an illiterate teenage farm girl, to quickly learn what she had to learn to deal as an equal with royalty, bookish clerics, and trained soldiers of high rank. Coupled with this genius there had to be phenomenal force of will. Her genius enabled her to quickly master the rudiments of military leadership despite her absolute lack of formal training. Her force of will empowered her, a peasant girl, to browbeat royal officials into granting her an audience with the Dauphin Charles—and, having won that audience, to persuade Charles to place her at the head of his army with a horse, a suit of armor, a sword, a banner, and an entourage of her own.

If intellect and willpower are qualities that can be inherited, then we can see Joan's capacities foreshadowed in her parents. Her father, Jacques d'Arc, was a peasant farmer of the village of Domrémy, but among the village peasants he was first among equals. He commanded such respect among his neighbors that he served in several official roles in the affairs of the village. It was he whom they chose to represent the village to the regional military commander in a tax dispute—the same regional commander Joan was to badger for an escort to Charles at the beginning of her quest.[1] Jacques, in step with the trend of the time toward increased personal initiative among the peasantry, petitioned for, and obtained, the right for his neighbors to take shelter in an abandoned nearby castle whenever brigand bands and warring forces threatened the village.[2] Jacques was thus a man of notable intelligence, responsibility, and enterprise among the peasantry. He died in sorrow within a year after his daughter died at the stake.[3]

Joan's mother, Isabelle, was a woman of superb character. She showed what she was made of after Joan's death. An illiterate peasant woman, she made her voice heard along with that of King Charles VII to demand a posthumous retrial for her daughter. Her pleas for justice eventually reached the pope in Rome and she lived to see her long struggle rewarded with Joan's exoneration.[4] If the potential for greatness can be passed in the genes from parents to child, or if it can be developed in a child by parental example, then Joan was well served in both her parents.

Nicholas Wright, in his recent book about the Hundred Years' War as fought in the French countryside, argues persuasively that Joan's childhood experiences tempered her for the life of a soldier and leader. Her father's role of commanding the local watch, and her own duties of helping to herd the village livestock to safety when hostile forces threatened the area, taught her lessons about collective action and personal responsibility in serving the common good in dangerous times.[5]

High intelligence under stress is necessary in a military leader. The strongest unambiguous evidence of Joan's amazing powers of mind comes from the transcripts of her trial for heresy. From January to May 1431, over sixty of the most learned clerics in English-occupied France subjected her to an almost daily barrage of questioning. Illiterate Joan had no one to represent her or speak for her but herself. After being pushed to mental exhaustion in court each day, she was pushed to physical and emotional exhaustion each night by sadistic prison guards who mocked and abused her.[6]

The learned clerics sought to trap Joan with trick questions of theology so that her own answers would condemn her. The illiterate peasant answered with such consistent brilliance that she made the clerics look like fools. She forced the mastermind of these odious proceedings, Bishop Pierre Cauchon, to move the trial from public chambers to closed chambers. Amazingly, Joan's superb answers found their way into the official record thanks to court scribes who sympathized with her.[7]

Specific examples of Joan's answers demonstrate her presence of mind under pressure. For example, she was asked if the saints who she claimed appeared to her hated the English. The trick in this question was that if

Joan said "yes," she would be claiming that saints of the Church hated a people who, in 1431, were still every bit as Catholic as the French. If she said "no," then she would destroy the credibility of her own mission to make war on the English. Joan adroitly answered of her saints, "They love that which God loves and hate that which God hates."[8] In another instance, she was asked if she was or was not in God's grace. If she said that she was, the clerics were ready to hound her for the sin of presuming to know God's mind. If she said that she was not, she condemned herself. She replied, speaking of being in God's grace, "If I am not, God put me there, and if I am, God keep me there." The brilliance of this answer "stupefied" the court, in the words of an eyewitness.[9] At still another point, Joan refused to answer a question because, she said, she had already answered the same question eight days previously. The scribe instantly said that she was mistaken. She challenged him to search back through the pages of the trial record. The scribe did so—and Joan was proven right. With a spunk that was incredible under the circumstances, she jokingly told the scribe that if he made such a mistake again, she would pull his ears.[10]

Joan's brilliance at her trial does not have a *direct* bearing on her skill as a military commander. Still, the ability to think quickly and creatively under conditions of horrific stress is essential in a successful leader of forces in battle. Joan's conduct at her trial proves that she had brains in abundance to quickly master the rudiments of the art of war with no prior training.

D'Alençon's testimony, supported by Jean Chartier's chronicle, that Joan "excelled" in placing the artillery may be misleading to people with no military experience.[11] Excelling in "placing" the artillery is not the same thing as excelling in operating the artillery. A modern-day general does not need to know the complex "switchology" of operating the ballistic computer of a state-of-the-art tank. The specially trained crewmen of the tank are paid to have that skill. The general only needs to know the capabilities and limitations of that tank in doing damage to the enemy as he moves and places that tank, like a chess piece, on the chessboard of the battlefield. Likewise, Joan did not need to learn the technical minutiae of how to mix gunpowder for her artillery. Rather, she quickly had to grasp how the big guns should be positioned on the battlefield to do the most damage to the enemy, for example, by shooting at the corners of square castle towers and at the center of round castle towers.[12] Joan had the innate intellect to rapidly acquire the moves of a battlefield chess master.

There may have been a social aspect as well as a tactical aspect to Joan's mastery of the relatively new force on the battlefield that was gunpowder artillery. Throughout the preceding centuries of the Middle Ages, right up to and including Joan's own day, noble birth was an absolute social prerequisite for anyone aspiring to a high leadership role on the battlefield (except, of course, for a certain inspired farm girl from Domrémy). Technical expertise had never been a highly valued trait in the scions of noble warrior families. Courage on the battlefield and courtly manners in the great hall of the castle had always held, and still held, higher esteem. The rub was that by Joan's day, gunpowder artillery was the component of European armies that was growing fastest in terms of both size and sophistication—and that technical expertise was an absolute necessity for the men who worked the guns. The "master gunners" of the day were not generally men of noble birth. They were men of the rapidly emerging bourgeoisie, who may have been lacking in aristocratic battlefield panache and courtly manners, but who possessed specialized technical skills that most nobles did not. It is fair to speculate that while most noble military leaders of the day understood the importance of the new gunpowder weapons, they may have felt disdain for the social inferiors who manned the guns and who were threatening the nobles' monopoly on military leadership. Joan would have had no such problem in her working relationship with her gunners. As a peasant and as a pragmatic person who was more concerned with what worked than with class distinctions, she may have been able to establish a rapport with the gunners more easily than her noble co-commanders.[13]

Joan's quickly acquired intellectual mastery of the fundamentals of the art of war seems to have gone far beyond her skill with artillery. When studying her campaigns at the remove of nearly six centuries, it seems as if she understood and followed what modern military professionals call the "principles of war."[14] Every modern army that serves a major power conducts its combat operations according to a body of "how to win" theory that it teaches to its rising leaders in military academies and staff colleges. This theory often includes a list of half a dozen or so pithily worded principles of war. Students at military academies and staff colleges are constantly exhorted to memorize and apply these principles as they plan and fight their future battles. The list of these principles is virtually identical from one major modern army to another. It is only in the last century that the military intelligentsia has codified the principles of war into formal lists. However, a study of military history shows that successful generals since Alexander the Great have understood the concepts underlying the modern principles of war and have applied those concepts either consciously or unconsciously. Even though the principles were written down only recently by military intellectuals, they were derived from a close study of the actions of great generals of the past. The famous British military historian and theorist J. F. C. Fuller receives the credit for first writing down the principles in their modern form during World War I. The United States Army adopted Fuller's list for its own use in 1921.[15] The principles are really nothing more than a handy modern summary of military common sense, as military common sense has been applied by great generals since the beginning of recorded history.

The men who wrote down the principles of war in their modern form, Fuller and his counterparts in other modern armies, intended the principles to have eternal relevance in the field of military theory. Students of military history consider the principles to have this eternal quality. This presumed eternal relevance of the principles enables military historians to use them to analyze any battle ever fought, whether that battle was fought yesterday or in 1429. As will be demonstrated, one of the key uses of the principles of war is as an analytical model that helps explain why the winners won and the losers lost the great battles of history.

It is necessary to describe the principles of war in detail and then to demonstrate how military historians have applied the principles to analyze battles that were fought long before the current version of the principles was written down. The present-day United States Army lists its principles of war as "objective," "offensive," "maneuver," "mass," "economy of force," "unity of command," "surprise," "security," and "simplicity." The United States Army considers "speed" to be a crucial subordinate component principle of the principle of the "offensive."[16]

The objective is simply the clearly defined goal that, if achieved, will produce victory. A general must be able to articulate to his subordinates the clearly defined goal that will produce victory if he wants to achieve victory.[17] The principle of the offensive states that if one side wishes to win, it must attack and attack successfully. The side that is on the offensive possesses the initiative; that is, the side that is on the offensive compels the enemy to react to it, rather than it reacting to the enemy. While standing on the defensive does have its momentary advantages, only offensive operations can force a war to its desired conclusion. For offensive operations to attain their fullest effect, they must embody the subordinate component principle of speed. For an attack to succeed, it must move faster than the enemy's defense is able to react to it.

The principle of maneuver embodies the art of moving one's different types of soldiers and weapons on the map and on the battlefield to positions of advantage over the enemy. This is the chess-playing aspect of war.

The principle of mass demands that every single soldier and weapon possible be brought together at one place at one time—the place and time that the commander deems decisive to overwhelming the enemy at his most vulnerable or most vital point. Economy of force is the reciprocal of mass. It means that the commander must employ only the minimum essential soldiers and weapons at all times and places that are *not* his chosen decisive time and place. It is impossible for an army to be strong everywhere at once. In order to achieve mass at his chosen decisive point, the commander must have the courage to stretch his forces thin every place that is not the decisive point.

The principle of unity of command demands that *one* soldier possess the final and absolute authority to make strategic and tactical decisions for an army. That one soldier in command may solicit as much advice from as many subordinates as he wishes, but, in the end, the final decision must be his alone.

The principle of surprise states that an attack delivered on the enemy at a time and place he does not expect will have its power multiplied several times over by virtue of the psychological shock that such an attack inflicts on an enemy. An unexpected blow always hurts an enemy far more than a blow he does expect, even if the size of the friendly force making the blow is the same. The principle of security is the inverse of surprise. Security embodies taking every precaution necessary to ensure that friendly forces are never surprised by the enemy.

The principle of simplicity is an acknowledgment that Murphy's Law is supreme on the battlefield. Anything that can go wrong with a plan of battle will go wrong thanks to garbled orders, human blunders, bad weather, unanticipated enemy moves, or whatever. The more complicated a plan is, the more likely it is to fall apart in the unpredictable chaos of battle. Simple plans violently executed work best.

The current British Army list of the principles of war is virtually identical to the American list, with the addition of two more: maintenance of morale and administration.[18] Maintenance of morale is the declaration that the soldier's will to fight is *the* essential precondition for victory. All the expensive state-of-the-art weapons conceivable are of no use if the soldier wielding those weapons lacks the inner courage and force of will to go forward into danger to confront his enemy. It is the first duty of a commander to nurture this courage and force of will in the hearts of his soldiers. The principle of administration recognizes that soldiers must be properly fed, properly clothed against the weather, properly supplied with the right types of ammunition and repair parts for their weapons, properly taken care of when wounded or sick, and, hopefully, properly paid. The job of managing all these administrative details is dull, tedious, tremendously difficult, and absolutely vital. History is full of generals who were brilliant at implementing the principles of objective, offensive, and maneuver, but who came to ruin because they were unable to keep their soldiers fed in a distant, desolate land.

A survey of the textbooks used to teach cadets at the United States Military Academy at West Point about military history demonstrates the use of the principles of war to analyze battles that took place centuries before the principles were written down in their present form. In the following quotations drawn from the series of textbooks called "The West Point Military History Series," italics highlight direct references to the principles of war in the course of analyzing past generals and battles. The volume on ancient and medieval warfare says of Alexander the Great's plan to surreptitiously cross the Hydaspes River, and thereby outwit the opposing Indian army, "The plan itself incorporated flexibility and *surprise,* and exploited the terrain to enhance *security."* The same volume says of Hannibal's crushing victory over the Romans at Cannae, "Once again, generalship, *surprise,* and *maneuver* resulted in an outstanding victory by a master tactician and general."[19]

The West Point volume on early modern warfare describes the duke of Marlborough's worries about divided command responsibilities in a coalition army. The volume goes inside Marlborough's presumed thought process to state, "For the coming battle there must be *unity of command."* A few pages later, the same volume says of Marlborough's victory at Blenheim, "Marlborough's plan had succeeded admirably. At the decisive point he had *massed,* fresh squadrons of cavalry and infantry battalions." When this volume comes to the campaigns of Frederick the Great, it judges Frederick's brilliant victory at Leuthen to be "a complete lesson in tactics—deception [read *"surprise"*], *maneuver,* inspiration [read *"maintenance of morale"*], and resolve—gathered together into a volume on generalship."[20] As these representative examples drawn from West Point textbooks demonstrate, the principles of war have been used as a heuristic device to gain access to the thought processes of great generals of the distant past. A more appropriate analytical use of the principles in historical study is to use them as a template by which the actions of a military leader of the past, such as Joan, can be assessed. Using the principles in this way will help illuminate the "how" of Joan's extraordinary military success.

In Joan's day, there were no committees of colonels sitting in army staff colleges thinking up catchy-sounding lists of the principles of war. Yet, it still remains true that the writing of treatises on the art of war began in ancient times. The writing of military theory continued through the medieval era, albeit with much less frequency than in the days of the Greeks and Romans. Military theorists of ancient and medieval times showed in their writings that they had a keen appreciation for the concepts that would become codified into the principles of war in the early twentieth century. The foremost piece of military theory written in Western Europe during the Middle Ages was *The Book of Deeds of Arms and of Chivalry*, written by Joan's contemporary, the great feminist author Christine de Pizan.[21]

Drawing heavily on the Greek and Roman classics, de Pizan wrote a cogent body of how-to-win theory for the military leaders of her day. Many of her pieces of advice clearly embody ideas that centuries later would be incorporated in the principles of war. When de Pizan wrote, "Surprises alarm the enemy.... No plans are better than those of which the enemy has no knowledge until they are carried out," she was obviously anticipating the modern principle of surprise.[22] When she cautioned her readers, "When you know that the enemy's spies are wandering around your army, make your men retire to their tents," she was anticipating the principle of security.[23] When she titled a chapter, "The Seven Ways of Drawing Up an Army for Combat, According to Vegetius," and when she filled this chapter with descriptions of various ways to arrange ranks and files of soldiers according to the situation, she was writing about the principle of maneuver.[24] De Pizan's advice to her martial readers—that they ensure their soldiers are properly paid, that they "distribute wisely" the "victuals" from the carts, and that they avoid setting up their camps near unhealthy marshes—demonstrated her appreciation for what became the principle of administration.[25] Finally, de Pizan's detailed treatment of what sort of speech a general should make to his army before battle, and the stress she placed on a general treating his men with benevolence, prove that she knew the importance of maintenance of morale as a principle of war.[26]

Successful commanders of Joan's time demonstrated that they understood the ideas that would become codified in the principles of war centuries later. At Agincourt, Henry V's complete personal control over his army exemplified the principle of unity of command. On the French side at Agincourt, the presence of several overly haughty nobles in the leadership, and their inability to properly discipline their army, showed a disastrous lack of unity of command. Henry's move to secure the flanks of his formation by butting them up against dense forests, and his arranging his men in mutually supporting blocks of dismounted knights and longbowmen, were fine displays of the principle of maneuver in practice. The inability of the French to attempt any move more sophisticated than a headlong, mad rush, straight at Henry's position, was a failure to exercise maneuver. At Patay, La Hire honored the principle of surprise when he was able to launch an attack from an unexpected direction at an unexpected time, thus rendering the English incapable of responding effectively and, thereby, reducing them to panic. At the same time, the English failed to honor the principle of security by their failure to have scouts of their own out combing the countryside to provide early warning of any French approach.

The writings of de Pizan and the actions of commanders such as Henry V and La Hire show conclusively that even if the principles of war were not written down as such until the early twentieth century, the concepts the principles embody were understood by, and acted on by, military leaders in the early fifteenth century. If nothing else, the battles just mentioned show that the principles of war, as written down in the twentieth century, have good predictive value when picking winners and losers in battles fought in the fifteenth century. It appears as if Joan picked up these basic ideas of military theory quickly as she rode side by side with the Bastard, d'Alençon, and La Hire down the dusty roads of France.

Joan's leadership of the army suggests that she especially honored the principles of maintenance of morale, objective, offensive, speed, maneuver, mass, and economy of force. Joan was the practitioner of maintenance of morale par excellence. She is without peer in all military history for her mastery of this principle of war. Her inspirational heroics at the Tourelles and elsewhere are an example for commanders of any era to emulate.

Joan had it easy with regard to the principle of the objective. Her voices from Heaven explicitly told her what her objectives were. (If it was not voices from Heaven telling her what her objectives were, then it was her intuitive genius for war telling her. Perhaps her voices and her intuitive genius were really the same thing.) In Joan's retrial, d'Alençon, royal court bureaucrat Simon Charles, and a cleric named Seguin de Seguin, who was one of her early supporters, all testified about her public pronouncements concerning her objectives. These three pieces of testimony overlap, partially agreeing with each other and partially contradicting each other. Reviewing the testimony, it is certain that Joan had at least two self-proclaimed objectives: breaking the English siege of Orléans and escorting Charles to Reims to have him properly anointed and crowned king of France. She may have had two more objectives: completely driving the

English from France and securing the release of the duke of Orléans, the Bastard's legitimate half-brother, from his captivity in England.[27] (See Appendix A.)

Two of Joan's objectives were purely military: breaking the English siege of Orléans and then driving the English completely from France. One of her objectives was political and symbolic: getting Charles anointed and crowned at Reims to sanctify his legitimacy as the true king of France and to show Henry VI of England to be nothing but an interloping pretender to the French throne. To the profoundly religious medieval mentality, such a symbolic act had tremendous power to motivate the part of the population that was loyal to Charles to even greater efforts on his behalf—and, conversely, to demoralize the pro-English faction.

It is worth digressing to explain and to emphasize the decisive importance of Joan's objective of having Charles anointed and crowned at Reims. The anointing of a French king at Reims had a mystical significance rooted in the very beginnings of French history. Clovis was the chief of the pagan barbarian tribe known as the Franks that settled in what was to become France during the collapse of the Roman Empire. In about 496 A.D., Clovis converted to Christianity and was formally crowned king of the Franks. By this act, the Franks became French, Clovis became the first king of France, and French history began. Clovis was crowned in Reims. According to legend, a white dove came down from heaven to deliver the vial of holy oil with which Clovis was anointed king. Every single king of France after Clovis was anointed from what was popularly believed to be the same miraculous vial of oil. What people sincerely believed to be this vial of oil was stored for safekeeping in Reims. Right up until Joan's day, and long afterward, no man could claim to be the true king of France unless he first journeyed to Reims to be anointed with the presumed holy oil during his coronation. Like everyone else in her day, Joan accepted the significance attached to this holy oil to be a literal truth. Hence her obsession with getting Charles to Reims as quickly as possible to have him anointed as part of his coronation. She understood that by the act of anointing Charles according to tradition, his legitimacy as the true king of France would become unassailable in the eyes of his supporters and also in the eyes of masses of people who had previously been uncommitted. In 1431, a few months after Joan died at the stake, the English brought the ten-year-old Henry VI across the Channel to be crowned king of France. The English tried to recapture the city of Reims with its vial of holy oil but failed. Young Henry was crowned king of

France in Paris instead—but, with the holy oil absent, the coronation was seen by all as an empty and ineffective gesture.[28] Joan was fully justified in the importance she attached to her political-symbolic objective of anointing and crowning Charles.

Joan's objectives drove her to seize upon the principle of the offensive. To drive the English from their positions surrounding Orléans, she could not passively sit inside the city walls and await attack. She *had* to go outside the walls and attack the English in their forts. To get Charles to Reims through 250 kilometers of enemy-held territory, she *had* to go on an offensive march of conquest. It is a miracle of military history that her offensive march was both successful and bloodless. Every single battle Joan fought was an attack of some kind.

Joan was always aggressive in honoring the principle of the offensive, but not mindlessly so. On the last day at Orléans, on the day before Patay, and at Montépilloy, she and her co-commanders refused to play the English game of charging headlong into prepared English field positions. The last day at Orléans, the day before Patay, and Montépilloy thus became nonbattles, with the armies marching away with little or no blood being shed. Joan was smart enough to let discretion rule over pure valor when the situation warranted it.

When Joan's attacks succeeded, as at Orléans, Jargeau, and Patay, it was largely due to her mania for the principle of speed. As she confided to Charles at the outset of her career, her voices had told her that she "would last but a year and a little more."[29] She was obsessed by the knowledge that she would have to work fast or fail. She knew that she must allow the English no rest between battles to recover and reorganize themselves. Therefore, she knew that she could allow no rest for herself or her army as she strove to maintain constant pressure on the English. When Joan's attacks failed, as at Paris, it was because Charles's procrastination had robbed her of her decisive moment when her enemies were most vulnerable. Charles's procrastination gave the English and Burgundians the time they needed to reorganize themselves, and so they were able to foil Joan's attacks when Charles again gave her free rein.

Along with maintenance of morale, speed was Joan's signature principle of war. When Joan told Charles that he would have her services for only about a year, she was trying to impress upon him that she would have only a year to achieve her objectives of breaking the English siege of Orléans, getting Charles to Reims, and then driving the English from the rest of France. Breaking the siege of Orléans, crowning Charles, and driving the

English out of France were Joan's strategic objectives. That is, breaking the siege, crowning Charles, and driving out the English were her macro-objectives by which she sought to win the Hundred Years' War. Again, she gave herself a year to accomplish these strategic objectives. In other words, she was giving herself one year to achieve strategic results of a decisive, war-winning quality that the rival military professionals of both France and England had been unable to achieve in ninety-two years. She knew she would have to work fast—she knew she would have to drive herself, Charles, and her army with relentless urgency—to achieve her unprecedentedly ambitious strategic objectives in the time allotted.

Strategic macro-objectives determine tactical micro-objectives. Tactical objectives must support the accomplishment of strategic objectives. Joan's tactical objectives were to seize, as quickly as possible, each of the key English fortified positions at the Tourelles, Jargeau, Meung, Beaugency, and any English-held towns that opposed her march on Reims. At each of these places, she violated the military conventional wisdom of her day that called for capturing fortified positions through the tactic of methodical sieges that could drag on for weeks. At each of these places, she eschewed the tactic of the methodical siege in favor of the tactic of the lightning-quick direct assault. As mentioned in the previous chapter, the direct assault was characterized by using scaling ladders, inspiring leadership, and brazen courage to storm up and over the walls to seize an enemy position in a single day. Because Joan knew that she had only a year to achieve her strategy for winning the war, she also knew that she simply did not have the time to spend on the tactic of methodical sieges at every English position she had to take. Her strategy of speed compelled her to employ the high-speed tactic of the direct assault at every opportunity.

Joan tied her tactics into her larger strategy. She not only stormed the fortifications at the Tourelles, Jargeau, and Meung using the tactic of the lightning one-day assault, but she also conducted these assaults one after the other as rapidly as possible to fulfill her larger strategic need for speed. She moved at high speed tactically by assaulting and storming each enemy position in a day at each individual location. She moved at high speed strategically by moving from each location to the next as rapidly as she could make her soldiers march—and as rapidly as she could persuade Charles to acquiesce in her plans. In a period of seven days, June 12 to June 18, 1429, Joan fought, and won, four critical battles at four scattered locations: Jargeau, Meung, Beaugency, and Patay. In accomplishing this feat, she established a whirlwind tempo of operations that was unprecedented for the Middle Ages. When Joan browbeat her co-commanders into an immediate assault on the Tourelles; when she spurred d'Alençon's resolve at Jargeau; when she exhorted d'Alençon, the Bastard, and de Richemont to press on to battle at Patay; when she urged Charles to "drag out his councils no longer" at Loches and Troyes; when she did all these things, she honored the principle of speed.[30]

Joan put on a tour de force of the principle of maneuver when she used the strategy of the central position to strike east from Orléans at Jargeau, then double back through Orléans to strike west at Meung and Beaugency. When she struck at Jargeau with every man, horse, sword, and gun she could put together, she honored the principle of mass. When, at the exact same time, she trusted the small garrison at Orléans to watch her back in the direction of Meung and Beaugency, she honored economy of force.

The maddeningly difficult question to answer is how much of the French army's successful use of the principles of war was due to Joan's brain and how much was due to the brains of her co-commanders working under the lash of her sense of urgency. At Orléans, it seems that the choice of which English forts to attack in which sequence was made by her co-commanders; but without Joan's constant goading and heroic behavior in the frenzy of battle, her co-commanders' plans would never have turned into action. By the time of the actions at Jargeau, Meung, Beaugency, Patay, and Troyes, it seems that Joan's intellect was the main driver of the French army's fine display of the principles of war in practice.

The principle of war that the French violated most is the principle of unity of command. The ad hoc French "committee" style of making decisions was a gross negation of this principle. From Orléans through the march on Reims, Joan was able to force the French committee system to work in spite of itself because of her ability to dominate her co-commanders, and the Dauphin, with the power of her personality. Immediately after the coronation in Reims, it all fell apart as Charles, with his circle of anti-Joan civilian advisors, came to loggerheads with Joan and her brother warriors. The result was the army being pulled this way and that as it slowly lurched from Reims toward Paris. At Paris, Charles, backed by his civilian advisors, aborted what could have been a successful operation had he given it proper support.

The French were also shaky in their application of the principle of administration, as evidenced by the fact that their soldiers went hungry during the days that Charles vacillated outside the walls of Troyes during the march on Reims. The French were lucky indeed that Joan's charismatic presence enabled the men to subsist on their enthusiasm for the cause, if only for a few days.

JOAN'S USE OF WORDS AND SYMBOLS TO MOTIVATE HER FOLLOWERS

Joan's ability to forcefully articulate what had to be done in the crisis of war was one of her great leadership attributes. Her stated conviction that God was guiding her had a hard-edged practicality to it that she expressed in a powerful way. She understood perfectly that God giving guidance was not to be confused with God doing the work. Before the Dauphin Charles gave his final approval for Joan to place herself at the head of the army, he had her questioned by a panel of learned clerics in Poitiers to ascertain whether she was, as she claimed, the virtuous instrument of God's will or a deceitful force of evil. Seguin de Seguin was a professor of theology who was on the panel at Poitiers. Years later, he gave his testimony at the retrial. He stated that one of the examining clerics at Poitiers had said to Joan that if God wanted to deliver the people of France from their troubles, there was no need of soldiers. Joan replied, "In God's name, the men-at-arms will fight and God will give them victory." This answer pleased the assembled clerics.[31] D'Alençon testified that he had had his doubts about the haste with which Joan ordered the assault on Jargeau. She gently reproved him with the words, "Do not hesitate!...Work, and God will work."[32] Joan's understanding that God's guidance had to be coupled with human deeds provided fodder for her cutting wit. D'Alençon described how the army leadership was divided over whether or not to attack Jargeau immediately. Urging the bolder course as always, Joan "added that if she was not sure that God was managing affairs, she would prefer to guard her sheep and not expose herself to such perils."[33] Joan's ability to forcefully express the view that God was on the side of the French but that the French had to earn God's help by their own exertion was yet one more aspect of her character that enabled her to pull the army along behind her.

The informal, ad hoc "committee" nature of the French military high command worked to Joan's advantage. In that system, forceful eloquence and strong character counted for more in councils of war than formal factors of rank and position.[34] Joan's era was a time when people of all social classes, even high-ranking military leaders sitting in war councils, were marked by intense religious faith. Joan's apparent direct connection to God, seemingly confirmed by her unexpected yet repeated victories, must have added immensely to her power to persuade.[35] Her gift for simple but powerful rhetoric only magnified what her cohorts wanted to believe was her divine authority. Even those few members of Joan's war councils who lacked faith themselves must have known that it was the religious faith that the masses of soldiers had in her mission that empowered the army to fight so well. Such nonbelievers as existed in French councils of war would still have feared to tamper with a proven formula for victory. Time after time, Joan took full advantage of all these factors to alternately plead, cajole, argue, exhort—and inspire—her nominal superiors to adopt her preferred course of action. After Charles's coronation, Joan's ability to impose her will on royal war councils rapidly diminished. Charles used the new sense of authority the crown gave him to undercut the authority of the soldier girl who had won him the crown. Nonetheless, by that point, Joan had already made her indelible imprint on history.

In 1981, the publication of the book *Joan of Arc: The Image of Female Heroism,* by Marina Warner, brought a new, radical—and persuasive—voice to the study of Joan's life.[36] Warner argues that Joan's impact on history was based on her ability to embody a number of different archetypes to which the people of her day responded in various ways. To her English enemies, says Warner, Joan embodied the archetype of the Harlot and the archetype of the Heretic. To her French friends, she embodied the idealized archetypes of the Ideal Androgyne, Knight, and Prophet. Warner maintains that by assuming these three roles for her French followers, and by playing these roles to the utmost, Joan pushed all the psychological buttons needed to win the loyalty of her people. If we accept Warner's argument, it becomes evident that Joan's acts of personifying the Ideal Androgyne, the Knight, and the Prophet, were key components of her military success.

Let us first consider the rubric of the Ideal Androgyne.[37] Joan always made it clear to everyone that she was a girl, not a boy. The feminine aspect of her identity was embodied in the title she proudly invented and gave to herself: "Jehanne La Pucelle," that is, "Joan the Maiden." But she was a maiden who wore men's clothes, who cropped her hair short, who rode a horse astride, not sidesaddle, and who forced her own way through the manly realm of action, not the womanly realm of domestic quietude. Even when she spent time at the royal court, far from the harsh necessities of life in an army camp, she still affected the appearance and mannerisms of the male. When at court, she took obvious delight in dressing up in the expensive, extravagant height of fashion for a young *man*. (In fairness to Joan, it should be remembered that the expensive, extravagant clothes she wore were all gifts from grateful admirers.)[38] Warner writes:

> Through her transvestism, she abrogated the destiny of womankind. She could thereby transcend her sex; she could set herself apart and usurp the privileges of the male and his claims to superiority. At the same time, by

> never pretending to be other than a woman and a maid, she was usurping a man's function but shaking off the trammels of his sex altogether to occupy a different, third order, neither male nor female, but unearthly, like the angels whose company she loved.[39]

As Warner points out, the prejudices of our own culture are such that a girl assuming the mannerisms of a boy is seen as "cute" and, in some ways, admirable. She is taking a step up in her condition; she is making herself into something bigger and better than "just a girl." A boy who assumes the mannerisms of a girl is vulnerable to scorn for taking a step down, for making himself into something less than he should be.[40]

By assuming male mannerisms *successfully,* while still being a girl beneath her male mannerisms, Joan was able to transform herself into something sexless but still endearing and worthy of respect. By turning herself into a unique sexless entity—an entity like a sexless angel—she was able to transcend the limits that people of her day imposed on mere girls. By turning herself into a sexless, angel-like entity, she won herself the credibility in people's minds to take command of an army, something no mere girl could ever do.

Turning to the archetype of the Knight, Warner states that Joan had the "ability to embody an urgent set of symbols, and it was not accidental that, having this gift, she chose the compelling idiom of chivalry and codified her mission in its language."[41] The leaders of the French army all subscribed to the ideals of chivalry (even if they fell short of those ideals in actual practice) and they all responded to the symbols of chivalry. Warner argues that Joan's "dash" and "gift for display" enabled her to embody the symbols of chivalry in her own person and thereby legitimize herself as a true knight in the eyes of the knights she led. Three of the symbols of chivalry that Warner keys on are the horse, the sword, and the banner. No man or woman could claim the title of "knight," and no man or woman could claim to embody the values of chivalry, unless he or she had a fine horse, a worthy sword, and a proud banner. Warner describes at length Joan's conspicuously superb equestrian skills and her sword and banner that were laden with symbolic meaning. By her mastery of the symbols of horse, sword, and banner, Joan was able to present herself as the epitome of the morally pure, chivalrous knight who fought to defend the weak and free the oppressed. By so doing, she legitimized herself as a peer worthy of respect in the eyes of the men she led into battle.[42]

In many cultures, in many times, swords, and weapons in general, were seen in purely utilitarian terms as tools for killing. But in medieval Europe, as in feudal Japan, the sword was a cult object. Every legendary hero, in a culture that worshipped legendary heroes, had to have a miraculous sword possessing special powers. Every hero with a name carried a sword that also had a name. King Arthur had his miraculous sword named Excalibur, and the mighty Roland carried his sword Durendal, its hilt encrusted with relics of the saints.

Joan used four different swords at different times in her career, three of which were mundane in quality. But one, her absolute favorite, was her miraculous sword, with which her personal identity was inextricably entwined in the minds of her followers. This sword was the sword of Saint-Catherine-de-Fierbois. After the Dauphin Charles agreed to place Joan at the head of his army, but before she actually set off to go fight, she sent a message to the staff of the church of Saint-Catherine-de-Fierbois. (Catherine of Alexandria was Joan's patron saint and the main "voice" that spoke to her.) The message asked the men at the church to dig down into the floor behind and in front of the altar. If they did so, said Joan's message, they would find a sword at one of the two places where they dug. She asked if they would please send this sword to her. The men at the church knew nothing about any such sword, but they did as Joan asked. They discovered a sword buried not very deeply behind the altar. The rust on the blade came off easily when they rubbed it. There were five crosses marked on the blade. People in the town of Fierbois and the city of Tours gave her two sheaths for the sword as gifts, one of velvet and the other of cloth-of-gold. Practical Joan ordered a heavy leather sheath for it.

The sword of Saint-Catherine-de-Fierbois became Joan's primary sword. Her supporters took her seeming clairvoyance in knowing where to look for the sword as a miracle. She herself stated at her trial that her voices had revealed the location of the sword to her. Joan's followers added their own embellishment to the story of the sword's origins: they said that the great French warrior hero Charles Martel had wielded the sword in his victory over the Saracens at the Battle of Tours in the year 732. With the miraculous sword of Saint-Catherine-de-Fierbois proudly buckled at her side, Joan aligned herself with the legendary heroes of the past in the minds of her followers. Her legitimacy as a military leader was thereby enhanced multiple times over.[43]

If having a miraculous sword helped Joan's cause, it could also, in a special instance, harm her cause. The retrial testimony of d'Alençon and the chronicle of Jean Chartier explain how this harm came about. One day, shortly after Charles's coronation in Reims, but before the attack on Paris, Joan indulged her habit of chasing prostitutes out of her army's camp. As usual, she brandished her sword at the women as she drove them before her. Then, she whacked one of the women across the backside with the flat of her sword—and the sword broke. Chartier claimed that though the armorers tried to repair the sword, they could not, thereby proving the sword's divine origin. No mere mortal could repair a sword made in heaven. Chartier added that when Charles heard how the sword had been broken, he was dismayed and scolded Joan for not using a stick on the woman instead. The evidence and accounts provided by other sources contradict d'Alençon and Chartier with regard to the sword, and Chartier's own chronology is confusing. It is therefore impossible to verify if Joan actually broke her sword at all, and, if she broke it, whether or not she broke it in the manner, time, and place d'Alençon and Chartier described. It is, however, chilling to note that the alleged breaking of the miraculous sword took place at the time when Joan's military fortunes changed from glorious victories to humiliating defeats. If in fact Joan broke her miraculous sword at the time and place d'Alençon and Chartier claimed, the effect on her confidence and the confidence of her army must have been catastrophic.[44] However, it is also worth speculating that d'Alençon and Chartier may have tried to explain Joan's change of military fortunes by inventing or embellishing the tale of how her sword broke.

Next on Warner's list of symbolic chivalrous items that Joan incorporated into her own persona is Joan's banner. Warner explains how the symbols on a knight's banner advertised to all his perception of himself and his role in the world. Joan testified at her trial how her voices had dictated the design of her banner to her. Her banner was an immense swallowtail of white cloth spangled with the three-petaled golden lilies that were the emblem of France: the fleurs-de-lis. At the wide part of the banner, near the staff, Joan ordered that there be painted an image of Jesus enthroned in heaven with an angel on either side of Him. Also painted on the banner were the words "Jhesus-Maria." When Joan was in battle, her huge banner, streaming behind her as she rushed forward, served the practical purpose of showing her men where she was and where she wanted them to follow. With its design that superimposed the lily emblem of France with the image and name of Jesus, her banner symbolically proclaimed the holiness of France's war for unity and freedom.[45]

By fully exploiting the symbolism of her sword and her banner, argues Warner, Joan made herself the ideal archetype of the Knight in the minds of the people who followed her. Joan's success in presenting herself as the living example of the ideal knight was crucial to winning the loyalty of her co-commanders and her soldiers.

Photo 7.1 This equestrian statue of Joan, located in Paris, is a fairly accurate depiction of her at the pinnacle of her martial glory. © The Art Archive / Dagli Orti.

The next archetype Warner identifies in Joan is that of the Prophet. As Warner points out, this is the archetype Joan felt uncomfortable with and would have preferred to do without. But after her prophecy of where her miraculous sword would be found came true, and after her numerous prophecies about the battles she would win and the wound she would suffer at the Tourelles became accomplished facts, the role of prophet became a role she could not shun. Joan's distaste for being a cult figure in her own person seems to have been genuine. During her enforced idleness after the attack on Paris, she spent some time as a houseguest of a gentlewoman named Marguerite La Touroulde. La Touroulde testified in the retrial that when Joan was staying with her, several local women had brought holy objects to her house, asking that Joan touch them. La Touroulde recalled that Joan had said to her with a laugh, "Touch them yourself, they will be as good from your touch as from mine."[46]

It is a historical truism that in times of intense and widespread chaos and suffering, such as the Hundred Years' War, people of all social classes hunger for the reassurance they can take from someone who seems to be in touch with the Divine. The people of France seized upon Joan's seeming gift for prophecy and forced her to fulfill the role of a prophet for them. Along with her fulfillment of the roles of Ideal Androgyne and Knight, Joan's fulfillment of the role of Prophet conferred upon her the public prestige she needed to carry out her program for France.[47]

In her recent doctoral dissertation titled "Heretic or Holy Woman? Cultural Representation and Gender in the Trial to Rehabilitate Joan of Arc," Jane Marie Pinzino lucidly amplifies some of Warner's ideas and makes some new key points of her own.[48] Some of her arguments are specifically relevant to Joan's military career. "The charismatic leadership of Joan," Pinzino argues, "was invigorated in part by her rhetorical appropriation of the medieval Christian holy war tradition. She drew upon the medieval ideology directed originally against the Muslims in Palestine, and applied it to the struggle of the French against the English in the Hundred Years' War."[49] In her chapter titled "The Standard Bearer," Pinzino describes how Joan was able to appropriate this crusading rhetoric. She explains the long historical process of how the Christian ideology of the holy war evolved—from applying only to crusades to free the Holy Land from the Saracens to also being applicable to morally justified wars fought by one Christian state against another. This process was complete by the time Joan came on the scene. Therefore, asserts Pinzino, when Joan undertook to arouse her countrymen's fighting spirits, she could adjust the earlier rhetoric of the Crusades to fit her purpose. She merely had to substitute the words "fighting for France" for "fighting for the Holy Land," and to substitute "English" for "Saracens." The French had developed a consciousness of themselves as being God's chosen people, so they were receptive to Joan couching the war against the English in terms of a crusade.[50]

In the same chapter of her dissertation, Pinzino relates the history of war banners bearing images of Jesus, Mary, or various archangels and saints. Joan was not doing anything new when she directed that the image and name of Jesus be put on her banner. Pinzino amplifies Warner's argument that by superimposing the lilies of France and the image and name of Jesus on her banner, Joan was making clear her belief that a war fought for France was a holy war, even if the enemy was every bit as Christian as the French. The mass population she inspired, and the loyal soldiers who enthusiastically followed her into battle, were eager to accept and to fight for this ideology. Again, the point is made that Joan's mastery of the use of symbols was critical to her military success.[51]

HOW JOAN'S COURAGE AND CHARISMA WON THE LOYALTY OF HER SOLDIERS

Beyond her intellect, which enabled her to quickly acquire rudimentary skills of command, and beyond the incredible force of will that empowered her to surmount all obstacles, Joan had innate qualities about her that made thousands of armed men *want* to follow her. The military has always been a man's subculture, regardless of the era and locale in question. Yet Joan, a young woman, was able to force her way into the boys-only club of the French military of her day and then to make that club her own. How did she manage to overturn the established order of military culture?

Men in military elites are jealously protective of their own elite status. They construct a daunting series of tests, both formal and informal, that anyone wishing to join their number must pass. In this, the warrior nobility of medieval France was a military elite like any other in history. Joan's ability to join this elite should have been crippled three times over: she was hardly more than a child, she was a peasant, and she was female. It is one of the miracles of her career that she was able to transcend these handicaps to become not only accepted but admired by the French warrior nobility of her day.[52]

The qualities that the members of a warrior elite demand in a new member are physical prowess, a willingness to cheerfully endure harsh living conditions, and, above all, physical courage of a sublime degree, which entails, among other things, carrying on in one's duties heedless of one's own wounds. All these qualities must be conspicuously displayed. Given Joan's triple handicap of her youth, social class, and sex, she had to display these qualities in awesome measure to win acceptance. As her warrior comrades testified in the retrial, she passed all these tests in grand fashion.

D'Alençon testified that the day after he first met Joan, he saw her astride a borrowed horse, practicing jousting with a lance at a target. He was so impressed by her natural ability that he gave her a fine horse as a gift.[53] The young knight Guy de Laval wrote glowingly about Joan's equestrian skills in a letter he sent home to his mother.[54] The gentlewoman Marguerite La Touroulde was, obviously, not a warrior herself, but she was keenly observant of the impression Joan made on military men. She testified that Joan "rode a horse carrying a lance as well as the best men-at-arms; and they admired her strongly for that reason."[55] Throughout her military career, Joan displayed amazing stamina in wearing a heavy suit of armor and staying in the saddle all day, day after day, sometimes even sleeping through the night in her armor. D'Alençon noted with approval that through the long weeks of her campaigns she "slept on the straw" as any soldier would without the least complaint.[56] The knight Thibault d'Armagnac testified that "all the captains admired her valor, her activity, and the pains and fatigues she endured."[57]

If there was a single event that clinched Joan's place as an admired, equal member of the warrior elite of France, it was when she took an English arrow through her shoulder at Orléans—and after the arrow was pulled out, she returned to the forefront of the fight with redoubled ardor. Hundreds of men saw her take that arrow and hundreds of men saw her come back, a bloodstain at her shoulder, her good arm waving her banner, her voice carrying over the din, shouting for one more assault. At that sublime moment she became forever *their* Maid and they became forever *her* soldiers. There is a still-extant chronicle called *The Life of Guillaume de Gamaches*. De Gamaches was a French knight who served in the defense of Orléans. According to *The Life*, when Joan first arrived in the city, de Gamaches called her "a little saucebox of low birth" in her presence and threatened to furl his banner rather than follow her. Mere days later, at the moment Joan was wounded, de Gamaches was one of the first to rush to her and stand over her to protect her. Speaking a deep apology, he offered his horse to carry her to safety.[58] Joan had what it took to make the most haughty warrior nobleman accept and then admire her.

After a military female has displayed the strength and courage to win the acceptance and respect of her male peers, the fact that she is a female may become an asset rather than a liability to her. When a military female has shown herself good enough to be "one of the guys," and if she retains a spirited, cheery, yet compassionate sort of feminine charm, the guys may find the juxtaposition of her masculine and feminine traits all the more endearing. Multiple pieces of evidence demonstrate that Joan had precisely that kind of charm.

A French government official named Perceval de Boulainvilliers, who met Joan, wrote a letter describing her to the duke of Milan. The letter described the mixture of masculine and feminine traits that fascinated and charmed de Boulainvilliers and innumerable other men who knew Joan:

> This Maid has a certain elegance. She has a virile bearing, speaks little, shows an admirable prudence in all her words. She has a pretty, woman's

voice, eats little, drinks very little wine; she enjoys riding a horse and takes pleasure in fine arms, greatly likes the company of noble fighting men, detests numerous assemblies and meetings, readily sheds copious tears, has a cheerful face; she bears the weight and burden of armor incredibly well, to such a point that she has remained fully armed during six days and nights.[59]

Before battle, Joan was ferocious in councils of war as she constantly demanded that the army attack. During battle, she was ferocious as she placed herself at the head of every assault, heedless of danger and her own wounds. But after battle, her tenderheartedness came out as she spent as much time weeping over the English dead as the French. In the aftermath of the Battle of Patay, she even held a dying English soldier's head in her lap to hear his confession and comfort him as he died.[60] To the warrior men of her inner circle, the cycle of her conflicting moods must have been exhausting—and endearing. She was strong and fierce when her men wanted a warrior comrade who was strong and fierce. She was gentle and kind when they most needed to be near a woman who was gentle and kind.

Frances Gies, in her *Joan of Arc: The Legend and the Reality,* further describes the natural charm that drew fighting men to the Maid. Gies points out that lowborn peasant girl Joan had the cheerful boldness to address the great noble d'Alençon with the familiar "tu" form rather than the formal "vous" form as would have been appropriate. Joan also, says Gies, kept up a "playful" rapport with d'Alençon, calling him her "gentle duke" and "pretty duke." Joan's use of "tu" and of these pet names for d'Alençon is confirmed both by d'Alençon's recollections and by the writings of his personal chronicler, Perceval de Cagny.[61] D'Alençon, by his own testimony, was enraptured by Joan from the moment he met her, and her informal playfulness must have been part of what charmed him. The squire Gobert Thibault testified that when he first met Joan, "she clapped me on the shoulder, saying that she would well like to have many men of my character."[62] It is easy to visualize Thibault blushing crimson—and being charmed out of his boots. In his often-cited letter to his mother, Guy de Laval gushed in his adoring descriptions of Joan. He wrote, "I went to her lodging to see her; and she sent for wine and told me that she would soon have me drinking in Paris; and this seems a thing all divine by her deeds, and also from seeing and hearing her."[63] Clearly, Joan was no somber, otherworldly little waif of a mystic. She had a bravado, a charm, and a winning manner that, combined with her proven strength and courage, made hardened fighting men adore her at the same time as they respected her.

Joan's female sexuality inevitably became part of the chemistry that drew men to her—but in a way that was the opposite of the norm. Her squire d'Aulon helped her into her armor every day that she was in the field and it was he who dressed her wounds. He testified that he often saw her naked legs and breasts and that "she was a young girl, beautiful and well-formed." D'Alençon said, "I slept with Joan and the men-at-arms on the straw; sometimes I saw Joan dress herself, and sometimes I looked at her breasts, which were beautiful." Yet, all of Joan's men, Jean de Metz, Bertrand de Poulengy, d'Alençon, d'Aulon, and Thibault—the men who slept on the ground beside her and saw her in her lovely nakedness—were adamant that they never felt carnal lust for her. Thibault elaborated that while they sometimes felt a carnal urge for Joan, they "never dared to express it to her." Thibault continued his commentary, saying of himself and his brother soldiers, "very often, if they were talking about sins of the flesh in terms to arouse their concupiscence, and they saw her approach, they could not speak like that anymore, but immediately abandoned their carnal impulses."[64]

Thibault's second comment proves that, with regard to ribald soldierly banter around the campfire, nothing has changed in 600 years.[65] Joan was remarkable in her ability to suppress this ribaldry, not because she was ugly, but in spite of the fact that she was beautiful. Her men saw a saintly goodness in her and it was shame that prevented them from making advances on her. They felt an exalted, pure love for her that they could not bear to sully with carnal words, much less deeds. She was not their paramour, but their angel. That indeed was the nickname the French army and the French people gave to Joan: "l'Angélique."[66]

De Metz testified that though he slept on the ground right next to Joan, he "was in such awe of her that I would not have dared to solicit her, and on my oath I declare that I never had any desire or carnal feelings." Yet, only a little bit later in his testimony, he proclaimed, "I was on fire with her words, and with what I believe was her divine love." Jean Barbin, a doctor of law serving the French Parliament, testified, "The men-at-arms considered her a saint."[67] It is no great stretch to suggest that, when young men encounter a beautiful woman who has won their respect to an extraordinary degree, their usual sexual lust may become sublimated into a devotion and loyalty that is passionate but chaste. Joan had the power to make thousands of armed men love her, not as an object of romantic desire, but as the living focus of their hunger to serve a higher cause. Whenever Joan rose in her stirrups to shout, "Let all who love me—follow me!"[68] she was exploiting a special relationship between leader and led that is unique in all history. Ultimately, it was this astonishing ability of Joan's to make an army of soldiers chastely love her—to the point that they would willingly face death in battle for her—that empowered her to bodily shove history onto a new path.

Chapter 8

JOAN'S LUCKY CIRCUMSTANCES: THE SECOND PART OF "HOW"

In addition to Joan's genius, courage, and charisma, there were more prosaic reasons for her winning ascendancy over people and events. It was a simple matter of the cliché about being in the right place at the right time coming true. Joan was lucky in that the conditions of her time and place gave her the opening to do what she did.

After decades of one humiliating defeat after another, both the military and civil leadership of France were demoralized and discredited. When the Dauphin Charles granted Joan's urgent request to be equipped for war and placed at the head of his army, his decision must have been based in large part on the knowledge that every orthodox, rational option had been tried and had failed. Even allowing for the religiosity of the time, only a regime in the final straits of desperation would pay any heed to an illiterate farm girl who claimed that voices from God were instructing her to take charge of her country's army and lead it to victory.

Long before Joan burst onto the public stage, the folklore of the French people included some prophecies that foretold a day when a young maiden would save France in its most desperate hour. Various versions of these prophecies included various details about this maiden; for example, she would come from Lorraine, or from a town near an oak forest, or she would come armed as a warrior. One of these prophecies was attributed to the legendary Merlin, while another was attributed to the Venerable Bede. Joan's home village of Domrémy was indeed near an oak forest on the Lorraine border, and her warrior prowess created an instant sensation among all loyal French people who saw her during her public career. Joan herself made mention of these prophecies when she was still an obscure farm girl trying to convince the people around her to take her seriously as the soon-to-be savior of France. A relative and a friend of hers, peasants like herself, each testified at the retrial about how Joan had pointedly reminded them of the prophecies. The masses of people Joan was coming to help sincerely believed in these prophecies, and this popular belief strengthened her cause.[1]

Proof of the power these prophecies had on the minds of the French people can be found in the writings of the great medieval feminist author, Christine de Pizan. De Pizan was a contemporary of Joan's and an ardent supporter of the French cause. In despair over the loss of so many of her courtly male friends at the Battle of Agincourt, she had retired to a convent. When she heard of Joan's incredible victories, she joyfully wrote a poem called *Ditié de Jehanne d'Arc* that glorified Joan and her achievement. In the thirty-first stanza of a poem that is sixty-one stanzas long, de Pizan specifically cited the prophecies of Merlin and Bede that found their fulfillment in Joan.[2] It seems that the prophecies about a girl in armor saving France helped make highly educated people such as de Pizan, as well as illiterate peasants, ready to embrace Joan when she came on the scene.

Another point that helped Joan win acceptance was the fact that women wearing armor and leading men into battle were *not* totally unknown. Two examples of militant women who were well known to the educated classes of late medieval Europe were Matilda of Tuscany and Jeanne de Montfort. Both these women were of high noble birth and both of them came from families of great political and military power. The deaths of Matilda's father, brother, and husband left her the sole heir to vast land holdings in northern Italy in the eleventh century. During the civil war fought in Brittany in the fourteenth century, Jeanne de Montfort's warlord husband was taken prisoner in battle by his enemies. These women suddenly found themselves in charge of feudal states—and both suddenly found themselves surrounded by rapacious male warlords eager to strip them of their inheritances. Both women won great fame by rising to the moment. They put on armor, mounted their horses astride, not sidesaddle, and led their loyal bands of male retainers in successful wars to defend their rights.[3]

The rare but famous examples of women such as Matilda of Tuscany and Jeanne de Montfort meant that the male political and military leadership of France was able to comprehend, and at least tentatively accept, the idea of a woman in armor, on horseback, leading men into battle. Even so, Joan must have put a severe strain on the paradigm established in the minds of the French leadership by the example of such powerful women. Not only was Joan female, she was utterly devoid of the noble blood that previous militant women of the Middle Ages had used to legitimate their claims to power.

The well-known examples of militant Biblical heroines such as Deborah, Judith, and Esther also helped the French leadership to reconcile themselves to accepting Joan's help. The famous and highly respected cleric Jacques Gélu wrote a treatise championing Joan and pointedly comparing her to the valiant Deborah. In common with every other literate person of the day who knew of Joan, Gélu expressed wonder at her and her exploits. Then he discerned God working through Joan in the same way He had worked through Deborah:

> This matter, although it remains marvelous considered in itself, that a woman, especially a girl or youth, because of the delicacy and modesty of their sex could fittingly be the leader of an army or surround herself with weapons and conquer warlike men who are powerful in body and accustomed to every terror, and conquer them; yet this should cause no surprise when considered in the light of the power of God, because He can bring victory among a few people or many equally, through a woman by His intervention as shown by Deborah.[4]

Joan was always equally adamant, though in far fewer words, that she herself was nothing but the tool through whom God worked. Christine de Pizan, in her verse paean to Joan, claimed that she exceeded Deborah, Judith, and Esther in the patriotic miracles God achieved through her efforts.[5] Whether or not Joan ever learned of these Biblical women of courage as she listened to homilies in church, she owed them a debt of gratitude for helping prepare her way in the minds of the educated social classes of France.

Joan was lucky in that the nature of armies and war in her time helped to magnify the effect of her style of inspirational leadership. The army she led contained only a few thousand men, not hundreds of thousands or millions as became the rule in the nineteenth and twentieth centuries. Her soldiers went into battle standing shoulder-to-shoulder in packed masses, not spread out to mitigate the effects of modern machine guns and high explosive. Her battles were fought out on battlefields that could be covered by a few football fields, as opposed to modern battles being fought across dozens of miles of Normandy beaches or hundreds of miles of Iraqi desert. All this meant that Joan's heroic inspirational exertions—charging ahead brandishing her huge banner, shouting encouragement—were seen and heard by the majority of her men at the exact instant that she was charging and shouting. The effect of her inspirational conduct was both palpable and instantaneous for her men. A modern-day general can only make inspirational speeches to his entire army via an assortment of electronic media; and most of his soldiers will probably only hear recorded versions of the speech after the battle is over. Any modern-day general who leaves his headquarters to put on a display of physical courage will be seen by only a tiny and insignificant percentage of his men. The story of his brave display will only seep slowly through the rest of his army. Joan was fortunate that the nature of armies and the nature of battle in her day ensured that her style of leadership would have the greatest possible impact.

Just as the conditions of her time magnified Joan's acts and words of inspiration, so too did existing conditions help her overcome her lack of formal military training. Armies of her day were vastly simpler than what they have become today. The war machine of the early fifteenth century contained far fewer and far simpler moving parts than the war machine of any subsequent century. Moving and placing units of a few hundred foot-mobile pikemen and archers and a few hundred horse-mounted knights, plus a few very simple cannons—all of them supplied from horse-drawn wagons—is one thing. Moving and placing units of tens of thousands of soldiers equipped with dozens of different types of complex rifles, machine guns, cannons, tanks, personnel carriers, helicopters, mines, antiaircraft missiles, radar sets, and so forth—all of it sustained by computer-based logistical systems of staggering size and complexity—is quite another matter. In Joan's day, a brilliant military amateur did not have an impossible amount of ground to cover in order to catch up with her professional comrades in arms. Today, a brilliant military amateur is merely someone who has the potential to do well as he or she progresses through the intense and protracted technical training required to turn him or her into a military professional.

Philippe Contamine, in his classic book *War in the Middle Ages,* describes the simplicity of the art and science of war as it existed in Joan's day. Military historians have conventionally regarded medieval times as a wasteland so far as military theory goes.[6] Military theory, so the conventional wisdom states, reached a high point with the ancient Romans and then atrophied until the Renaissance. The ancient Roman military theorist Vegetius was highly regarded by those few medieval warlords who chose to read his book *Epitoma de re militari.* The only noteworthy work of military theory written in Western Europe during the Middle Ages was by

Christine de Pizan, and she essentially copied Vegetius, making changes as needed to make him more relevant to a medieval readership.[7] The problem was that Vegetius wrote his theory to be applicable to the utterly professional standing armies of ancient Rome, while the armies of de Pizan's and Joan's day were only starting to transform themselves into something more than feudal armed mobs. As Contamine notes, there were no military academies in medieval Europe. The military professionals who were Joan's co-commanders learned what they knew about the art of war by hard experience as they served their warrior apprenticeships in the field.[8]

Joan served a warrior apprenticeship just as her co-commanders had already served before she came on the scene. The difference was that Joan's apprenticeship was far more compressed in time than those of her co-commanders. Fortunately for her cause, Joan possessed the innate mental gifts to learn what she had to learn about the art of war with amazing speed. Still, the simplicity of the art of war as it existed in her day was the essential precondition for her to pick up that art so quickly. So far as mastering even the rudiments of the art of war is concerned, Joan could only have done what she did in the medieval period in which she lived.

Joan was also lucky in the men who became her intimate comrades in leading the army. Her coterie of co-commanders—d'Alençon, the Bastard, La Hire, de Richemont, de Xaintrailles—represented a younger generation of French military leaders who realized that they had to do *something* different to overturn years of French battlefield defeat and humiliation. These men had already won some minor successes before Joan arrived.[9] They were men who were willing to give Joan a chance, whereas the previous generation of French military leaders, whose arrogance and incompetence had led to ruin at English hands, might well have scorned her. Joan's moral inspiration, force of will, and peasant outsider's pragmatic drive to do what worked were the catalysts these men needed to make their efforts attain their fullest effect.

It was in her first battles around the besieged French city of Orléans that Joan worked her first seeming miracles of military leadership. These miracles seem a bit less miraculous in that the English inadvertently helped Joan at Orléans by the faulty way in which they deployed their forces. The English grouped their men at Orléans in small packets in forts—the Augustins, the Tourelles, and others—that were spread around the city out of supporting distance of each other. This left the English vulnerable to a French counteroffensive. The English took up such a deployment simply because they did not have enough men to set up a continuous line of troops completely encircling the city. The English were willing to employ this less-than-ideal method because of their confidence in their own invincibility and also due to their belief that the French lacked the will to come out of the walls of Orléans to fight them.[10] The French high command and soldiers at Orléans could have done what Joan did at any time before she arrived but, as the English knew, they lacked the will to do so. Joan had to give the French the will to fight before they *did* make the attacks that they always *could have* made.

Chapter 9

SUMMATION

Genius, force of will, the ability to make thousands of soldiers follow her out of love, fortuitous circumstances—all these things enabled Joan to do what she did. And yet, every analysis of Joan must end with the admission that there is something about her that will be forever beyond our grasp. The facts of "what" she did seem beyond dispute; but the "how" of what she did can never quite be adequately explained in purely rational terms. It is insurmountably true that there are some things about her that we can contemplate in awe but that we cannot fully comprehend. She is the greatest case of "go figure" in all of history. As Katherine Anne Porter wrote in her foreword to Régine Pernoud's *The Retrial of Joan of Arc,* "She is unique, and a mystery, and as you read about her and think about her life, you are led up to a threshold beyond which she eludes you, you cannot cross it."[1] Whether Joan's leadership role was that of an inspirational mascot or a true battle commander or something in between, whether she was propelled by her own will and genius or was in fact guided by some force beyond material explanation, one thing will always be clear: Joan was exactly what she needed to be to bring her people victory.

Appendix A

JOAN'S FOUR KEY MISSIONS OR PROPHECIES

When reading the firsthand accounts of people who knew Joan, it becomes difficult to disentangle what she considered to be missions of hers—those that she felt impelled to achieve herself—from what were merely prophecies she made about events that would come to pass. The retrial testimony of those who knew her is both partly overlapping and partly contradictory on the topic of missions and prophecies. The best way to attempt to make sense of it all is to construct a sort of itemized program, such as that which follows.

I. In his retrial testimony, Simon Charles, president of the chamber of accounts of the government of Charles VII, stated that Joan declared that she had two missions when she first arrived at Chinon:[1]

1. Break the English siege of Orléans.
2. Lead the Dauphin Charles to Reims so he could be anointed and crowned king.

Joan achieved both these missions in her lifetime.

II. In his retrial testimony, Seguin de Seguin, one of the friendly clerics who questioned Joan at Poitiers, stated that Joan had proclaimed, not four missions, but four prophecies:[2]

1. The English siege of Orléans would be broken.
2. The Dauphin Charles would be anointed and crowned king at Reims.
3. Paris would return to Charles's rule.
4. The duke of Orléans would return from his captivity in England.

The first two prophecies came true in Joan's lifetime, largely through her efforts. The second two prophecies came true after she died, but her efforts during her lifetime laid the groundwork for the second two prophecies coming true.

III. In his retrial testimony, the duke of Alençon, one of Joan's closest military companions, stated that Joan had publicly declared that she had four missions:[3]
1. Drive the English out of France.
2. Lead the Dauphin Charles to Reims so he could be anointed and crowned king.
3. Free the duke of Orléans from English captivity.
4. Break the English siege of Orléans.

The second of four missions remembered by d'Alençon matches the second of two missions remembered by Simon Charles. The fourth of four missions remembered by d'Alençon matches the first of two missions remembered by Simon Charles. What d'Alençon remembered as four "missions" matches what de Seguin remembered as four "prophecies" if one changes the order of them and substitutes "driving the English out of France" for "Paris returning to Charles's rule."

Going by d'Alençon's list, Joan achieved the second and fourth missions in her lifetime and laid the groundwork for the first and third to be achieved after her death.

Appendix B

JOAN OF ARC AT THE MOVIES

Joan of Arc has been the subject of over a dozen feature films, the first of them made in 1897.[1] In this essay, I will present my personal assessment of all Joan of Arc movies that are easily available on VHS videotape and/or DVD in the United States.

I have two criteria by which I judge the worth of a movie about Joan of Arc. I give these criteria equal importance.

One criterion is a movie's fidelity to historical fact. In other words, does the scriptwriter of the movie have his actors say and do things that Joan and her contemporaries really said and did? Or does he take liberties with the facts of history in what I see as a misguided attempt to "improve" the story for dramatic purposes? (I regard the purely factual record of Joan's life to be so extraordinary that any attempt to "improve" on it is folly.) Further, are the weapons, armor, battle scenes, costumes, interior sets, and other details faithful depictions of what all these things looked like, according to what we know from historical records? Or does the movie look like the prop man raided the closet of some high school drama club?

My other, and equally important, criterion is how well or how poorly the leading actress interprets the character of Joan. We have abundant historical evidence in the writings of people who knew Joan, and in her own words as recorded at her trial, to be able to form a reliable image of her personality. Does the actress succeed or fail in drawing on this evidence as she plays the part? (Admittedly, the scriptwriter and the director have a large influence on how the actress interprets Joan's character.)

Here then follows my informal, personal assessment of selected movies about Joan of Arc.

JOAN THE WOMAN

Released in 1916. Black and white, silent. Directed by Cecil B. De Mille. Geraldine Farrar as Joan. Screenplay by Jeanie Macpherson.

While some movies of the silent era are creative masterpieces even when looked at with today's sensibility, this movie is a "turkey" now and, I suspect, may have been something of a turkey when it was released. The acting is of the overblown, artificial Victorian sort that was prevalent in too many early movies.

The movie is a typical Cecil B. De Mille "cast of thousands" extravaganza with huge battle scenes, a massively staged coronation scene, and so forth. The movie does present the narrative of Joan's whole life and career in a manner that, for the larger part, respects the historical record. However, details of armor and weapons are ludicrously bad, indicating a truly sophomoric props department. (Again, this is typical of the time when the movie was made.) Also, the way the movie makes heavy political and psychological references to the then-current events of World War I in France badly dates this movie's interpretation of the meaning of Joan's life.

Geraldine Farrar was a reasonably competent actress, but in the movie she looks fortysomething years of age and overweight as she tries to portray a teenage girl who possessed magnificent athletic ability. This is what finally puts this movie in the "don't-need-to-see-that-again" pile for me.

THE PASSION OF JOAN OF ARC

Released in 1928. Black and white, silent. Directed by Carl-Theodore Dreyer. Maria (Renée) Falconetti as Joan. Screenplay by Carl-Theodore Dreyer in collaboration with Joseph Delteil.

This is a silent-era movie that *is* a brilliant artistic masterpiece, even when viewed with eyes of 2003. The brilliance of Falconetti's acting, relying solely on facial expressions and gestures, is astounding. The actors who portray her trial judges are superb in the same way. Dreyer's use of tight close-ups of his actors' faces builds up a level of intensity that leaves the viewer cringing. Critics rightly call this one of the greatest silent movies ever made and perhaps one of the greatest movies of any kind.

While acknowledging the brilliance of director Dreyer and actress Falconetti, this movie fails to make it with me regarding historical veracity. The movie only covers the trial and execution of Joan, with no depiction of Joan's military career. That in itself is no problem for me. The scriptwriter clearly used the transcript of Joan's trial to write the script and that is commendable. However, starting with the little details and working up to the big issue, this movie has serious faults in its depiction of a historical event. The helmets, belts, belt buckles, and jackets of the English soldiers guarding Joan are obviously modified surplus items from the World War I period. We see Joan getting her hair cut with a modern pair of scissors. We see one of the clerics wearing modern eyeglasses. These blatant anachronisms distract the knowledgeable viewer from the true merits of the movie. But these are little points. The truly serious historical fault of this movie is its depiction of Joan's character.

Falconetti is breathtaking in acting out her interpretation of Joan's character, but in my opinion her interpretation is mistaken. She portrays Joan as being in despair and constantly weeping during her trial. My reading of Joan at her trial is that she was all dry-eyed *defiance* as she boldly answered her accusers and psychologically bludgeoned them. She was tough and confrontational at her trial, not broken down as Falconetti portrays her.

A nice bonus of this movie is that at the very beginning the camera gives us a close-up of the original and authentic pages of the transcript of Joan's trial. Those who buy the recently restored version of this movie in its newest incarnation on VHS videotape and DVD will also get to enjoy the beautiful new soundtrack music composed by Richard Einhorn.

JOAN OF ARC

Released in 1948. Color, sound. Directed by Victor Fleming. Ingrid Bergman as Joan. Screenplay by Maxwell Anderson and Andrew Solt.

In terms of historical veracity, this movie is the standard of excellence by which all other movies about Joan must be judged. The key episodes of Joan's life—her plea to the local military governor to send her with an escort to Chinon to see the Dauphin, her first meeting with the Dauphin, her great battle at Orléans, the coronation, her betrayal, and her trial—are all here and faithfully rendered. This movie was obviously made inside a studio and not out on location; nonetheless, the accuracy of the weapons, armor, costumes, battle scenes, and so forth ranks with the best that the film industry has ever produced. The suit of armor worn by Bergman shows fine workmanship and is the most accurate vision of the real Joan's armor in film. From the diagonal stripe on the coat of arms of the Bastard of Orléans to the scarred face of the one-eyed duke of Luxembourg, this movie gets the details *right*.

This movie also has good historical veracity in its portrayal of the major players in Joan's career. Charles is well portrayed in his weakness and indecision. The duke of Alençon's personal devotion to Joan is also well shown. While more recent movies have wrongly attempted to portray the chief judge at Joan's trial, Bishop Cauchon, as a basically decent man who was trying to do what he thought was right, this movie accurately portrays him as an amoral swine who would commit any crime in his vendetta against Joan. Joan's insistence on good moral conduct in the soldiers of her army is better portrayed in this movie than in any other. This is the only movie about Joan that effectively depicts the heartbreaking scene when she had to say farewell to her beloved co-commanders after King Charles ordered the army disbanded.

We know from the original documents of Joan's time that she was a young woman of superb wit with a gift for punchy one-liners. This movie draws on this known feature of Joan's character, as when Bergman proclaims that she must go to see the local military governor even if she has to wear her legs down to the knees with walking to his castle. (This saying of Joan's about wearing her legs down to the knees with walking comes straight out of the firsthand accounts of Joan by those who knew her. However, this movie has her say this about going to see the local military governor when in fact she said this about going to see the Dauphin at Chinon.)

My problem with this movie is Bergman's interpretation of Joan's character. To me, Bergman plays Joan as entirely too sweet and too deferential to the powerful people around her. We know that Joan had a strong personality that enabled her to argue her opinions with great force, sometimes angering those who listened to her. Bergman fails to convincingly convey Joan's sometimes overbearing character.

We know that Joan was emotional with pronounced mood swings. She was ferocious when she was a warrior *in* battle. But *after* battle, she became a tenderhearted child as she wept over English dead and French dead alike. Bergman does a good job weeping after battle, but she is not convincing as a fierce warrior in battle. One of the key moments of Joan's career was when she was shot through her shoulder by an arrow in the fighting outside of Orléans—and, after the arrow was pulled out, quickly returned to the most intense part of the fight to lead her men to victory. In my opinion, Bergman plays the vital arrow-pulling scene in a limp manner.

The bottom line for this movie is that its historical veracity is second to none but that Bergman gets Joan right only about half the time.

SAINT JOAN

Released in 1957. Black and white, sound. Directed by Otto Preminger. Jean Seberg as Joan. Screenplay by Graham Greene, adopted from the play *Saint Joan* by George Bernard Shaw.

This movie is a filmed adaptation of the live stage play of the same name by George Bernard Shaw. As such, it depicts Joan's entire career, but big battle scenes are omitted in favor of thought-provoking dialogues. This is all very fine, yet this movie fails to win my approval.

With regard to historical veracity, it was Shaw, in his stage play, who originated the myth that Bishop Cauchon was a good man who did what he thought was right—and who tragically came into conflict with Joan on matters of sincerely felt principle. In fact, he was a wretchedly evil man who engineered Joan's officially sanctioned murder. This movie, being adapted from Shaw's play, contains this inaccurate depiction of Cauchon.

Continuing with concerns of historical veracity, the costumes, armor, and so forth look halfhearted and as if they were made on a low budget. Charles is portrayed as a childlike imbecile when in fact he was a clever, if spineless, political manipulator.

Jean Seberg's portrayal of Joan leaves me cold. She plays Joan as a ditzy airhead completely dependent on the momentary promptings of her divine voices.

This movie's sole merit is the way Shaw's dialogue illuminates a number of philosophical themes.

APPENDIX B

JOAN THE MAID

Presented in two parts, *The Battles* and *The Prisons*. Released in 1993. Color, sound. In French with English subtitles. Directed by Jacques Rivette. Sandrine Bonnaire as Joan. Screenplay by Christine Laurent and Pascal Bonitzer. (This review refers to the cut-down, two-tape version available on VHS videotape in the United States.)

The makers of this movie have achieved the impossible. They have taken one of the most thrilling human lives in all of human history and made it boring. Flat, limp camerawork and flat, limp acting produce this sorry result.

Rivette displays close to zero imagination in selecting his camera angles and in moving his actors about. His camera seems permanently stuck in a middle-distance point of view inside of which his actors sometimes move but often just sit or stand. He has Bonnaire walk to one side of a room, turn, pose, deliver a couple of lines, walk to the other side of the room, turn, pose, and deliver a few more lines, while all the other characters in the scene remain practically motionless. I would expect more animation from a set of cutout paper dolls. Some instances of Rivette's camerawork leave me drawing a blank as to what effect he was trying to create. In one instance, he focuses his camera on the masonry steps of a spiral staircase. We see a group of his characters descend through the section of staircase we are looking at and disappear from view—then the camera remains glued to the same view of the empty staircase for long and useless empty seconds.

While Rivette's camera work is uninspired, so are all his actors, both major and minor. They deliver their lines in a listless monotone. They seem to be as bored with the proceedings as the audience.

The historical veracity of this movie is an odd mix of the superb and the inadequate. The script makes more and better use of straight quotations from the original documents of Joan's own time than any other movie about Joan ever made. Massive blocks of dialogue are lifted verbatim from the eyewitness accounts of Joan's contemporaries, in which they set down both her words and their own. The serious scholar viewing this movie wants to feel joy at hearing Joan's authentic words so faithfully echoed on screen and in actual French, not English—but his joy is canceled by his disappointment at the lifeless way in which these authentic words are delivered. Spoken lines that should resound with courage, purpose, sorrow, or defiance fall flat.

The visual aspect of this movie's historical veracity likewise mixes faithfulness with bungled presentation. This movie was filmed out on location among beautifully weathered, authentic old stone buildings and in pristine natural countryside. This gives it a delightfully correct visual feel when the camera is merely panning across a static scene. Also, this movie anticipates a subsequent movie about Joan, *The Messenger* (1999; see review below), in the detail with which it visually depicts anecdotal scenes from Joan's career that were described in the accounts left by Joan's companions. For example, we see Bonnaire as Joan having to wrestle her banner away from a momentarily confused friendly soldier as she leads the final attack at Orléans. For another example, we see the gruesome death of one of Joan's personal attendants at the attack on Paris. As with the quotations of Joan's actual words in the script, the value of these historic scenes is negated by their tepid depiction on screen. The battle scenes of this movie are pathetically underpopulated, weak, inept, and unconvincing. Cecil B. De Mille did a far better job with his battle scenes seventy-seven years earlier. Bonnaire's suit of armor is the cheapest, shoddiest, and phoniest ever made for a movie about Joan.

Seeing this movie all the way through is a numbing exercise in watching a magnificent opportunity be thrown away by a weak, apathetic effort.

JOAN OF ARC

Television miniseries broadcast by CBS in 1999. Color, sound. Directed by Christian Duguay. Leelee Sobieski as Joan. Screenplay by Michael Alexander Miller and Ronald Parker. (This review refers to the two-tape "directors cut" available for purchase on VHS videotape, not the cut-down, single-tape edition available for rent. The DVD version also contains the full "director's cut.")

The bad news is that this movie does repeated and gross violence to the facts of history in a way that leaves me gasping in horror and rage. The good news is that this movie is superbly directed with camera angles, cuts between points of view, and compositions of scenes for the camera that are acts of creative genius. Filmed on location among authentic medieval buildings in Europe, this is the most visually beautiful Joan of Arc movie there is, to the point of making my eyes mist over as I watch favorite scenes again and again. The *great* news is that Leelee Sobieski is the best Joan I have ever seen.

Let me talk about the bad things first. This movie, following in the Shaw tradition, portrays Bishop Cauchon as a good man whose sincere convictions put him on a tragic collision course with Joan. This movie goes beyond the pale by showing Cauchon and Joan having sometimes friendly, sometimes contentious discussions about theology while Joan is enjoying the height of her success *before* she was taken prisoner. This may be good drama but it is horrible history. Cauchon was an evil man obsessed with destroying Joan in any way possible *and* the two of them never met until Joan was already a prisoner of war. This movie shows Joan passively surrendering herself to her Burgundian enemies as part of some divinely demanded act of self-sacrifice. Nonsense. The real Joan fought ferociously as she was bodily toppled off her horse by enemy soldiers in the middle of a fierce and all-out battle. This movie shows Joan having a bitter falling out with one of her comrades in arms, Captain La Hire, before the assault on Paris. Didn't happen, folks. All of Joan's brother soldiers maintained intense personal loyalty to her for as long as they were together. This movie shows a nun as Joan's page, helping her into her armor. Nope. It was a boy who had that job.

The movie's historical inaccuracies persist in the little details. Much of the armor and weapons seen in use are from different time periods and different parts of the world than Joan's France. Sobieski's suit of armor is superbly made and is the most beautiful rendition of Joan's armor in film, but it is fancier than the armor of the real Joan and comes from a slightly later historical period. While all the other buildings depicted are authentic period buildings in Europe, the English fort of the Tourelles looks sadly cardboard. This movie shows the fighting at Orléans and Joan's trip to the stake taking place under an overcast sky with occasional little flurries of snow. While this makes for a tastefully somber vision of events, the fact is that both the battle and the execution took place in May. The movie shows Joan as upset with La Hire because he is thinking only about fighting the English at Orléans, not about bringing food supplies to the starving people of the city. Actually, it was the other way around. The French military leadership at first envisioned only pushing a supply convoy through to

Orléans—it was Joan who insisted on enlarging the mission to a full-scale offensive. The script does not give Sobieski enough to do at the Battle of the Tourelles. We see her observing the battle from astride her horse in a detached way when she should be scurrying around shouting encouragement. The script has Sobieski cheerful and exultant after the battle when the real Joan was weeping over the dead.

This version of Joan's story does get a few historical points right. The ultimatum to the English that we hear Sobieski dictating to a scribe is taken verbatim from the authentic document. Charles is well portrayed as clever and slimy. The relationship that Sobieski establishes with the Burgundian noblewoman played by Shirley MacLaine is based on fact.

Turning to the plusses of this movie, director Duguay's camerawork is some of the most magnificent that I have seen in any movie on any topic. He has a gift for quickly intercutting close-ups between characters who are witnessing the same event unfolding before them from different points of view—and who display different emotions on their respective faces. His close-ups of Sobieski brilliantly illuminate by turns this Joan's spiritual radiance, implacable determination, righteous disdain for those who fail to measure up to her standards, pure-souled bravery in crisis, joy in victory, and stoic resignation in defeat.

Duguay is equally a master of the distant shot that creates a tableau in motion of a great event as it is occurring. His naturally flowing views of Joan and her warrior entourage galloping their horses to battle and of a great army ranging itself for its greatest struggle are purely lyrical. Given that this movie was made for television, the gore in the battle scenes is restrained but the chaos and swirling motion of battle is superbly rendered. (Joan's famous arrow wound at the Battle of the Tourelles *is* replicated with full, emotion-churning displays of blood, both fresh and red and caked and blackened.)

When Sobieski is not having to cope with a flawed script, she makes a superb Joan. To begin with, she is Joan's age. Much more importantly, Sobieski beautifully captures the reserved but intensely forceful character that we know Joan had from contemporary descriptions of her. People on a mission from God do not have any fluff in their personalities. When Sobieski speaks, it is always with a purpose. In moments of peace, she *does* have radiant smiles and warm words for family and friends. But in moments of crisis and decision, especially when she is first establishing her reputation, she browbeats military leaders and court bureaucrats alike to bend them to her will. One of Sobieski's strongest scenes is her final conversation with Charles—the scene in which she knows that he is about to betray her. Sobieski masterfully uses a deadpan delivery to create a veneer of respect for her king over words that drip with sarcasm and disdain.

Sobieski performs by far the best scene of Joan having the arrow pulled out of her shoulder of any that I have watched. She is bravely in pain without being either limp or hysterical. At her trial, Sobieski conveys Joan's air of indomitable defiance better than any other actress I have seen. (I just wish the script made more use of the original trial transcript.)

A saint is supposed to glow. In certain key close-ups, Sobieski glows.

Watch this movie for its visual beauty and above all for Sobieski's excellent performance. Then watch the Ingrid Bergman version again to get your historical head back on straight.

THE MESSENGER

Released in 1999. Color, sound. Directed by Luc Besson. Milla Jovovich as Joan. Screenplay by Andrew Birkin and Luc Besson.

This is the most problematic and controversial movie about Joan of Arc ever made. With the exception of one particularly graphic scene, which I will describe later, this movie has superb fidelity to the external *facts* of Joan's life. However, this movie vaults recklessly into dangerous territory in the *interpretation* it makes of Joan's internal character and her motivations.

All previous movies about Joan have treated her voices as she would have wanted them treated—as plain and clear revelations from God that should be regarded with due reverence. *The Messenger* is a radical departure in Joan movies by treating her voices as the self-delusions of a young woman who was traumatized by a horrible experience in childhood and who embarked on her military career out of a thirst for revenge, not out of obedience to divine guidance. This movie shows an off-balance Joan trying to delude herself that her crazed, internally driven quest for revenge is in fact supported by guidance from God—only for her self-delusion to collapse as she faces the stake and can deny her true motivations in life no longer. *The Messenger* is thus a movie calculated to infuriate people who cherish the traditional view of Joan's life—that her voices were in fact honest guidance from the great beyond and that her voices were her strength and refuge, not her curse, in her last hours.

Turning to how this movie treats the *facts* of history, the battle scenes are magnificently realistic orgies of mayhem and gore. (Some of the weapons are a bit fanciful though, such as the masonry tubes the English use to roll stones down on the French attackers.) The visual depiction of the layout of the English fort of the Tourelles, just outside the city of Orléans, is absolutely the best that has ever been done (even if the outermost wall is shown as stonework when the original was probably earth and timber). I give this movie high marks for how it depicts Joan taking the arrow through her shoulder at the Tourelles and another arrow through her thigh at Paris. (However, the movie shows Joan returning to the attack on the Tourelles the morning after she is wounded instead of the same day as really happened.)

This movie shows various anecdotal scenes from Joan's military career that no other movie, save Rivette's boring opus, shows completely—scenes that were described in detail by eyewitnesses and recorded by history. For example, Joan has her last ultimatum to the English delivered by tying it to an arrow shot into the English fort of the Tourelles. (As with the Sobieski version, we hear Joan dictating this ultimatum using the words of the authentic original almost verbatim.) For another example, Joan's co-commanders at Orléans launch their first attack on the English without telling her about it. We see Milla Jovovich as Joan taking a nap in her quarters and then sitting bolt upright as her voices tell her that the battle has started without her. She rousts her sleeping squire and page to arm her. Running downstairs and out into the street, she vaults onto her horse and shouts to her page to hand her banner to her through the second-story window, which he does. She then gallops off through the streets to join the battle. This scene in the movie follows exactly the written accounts left by Joan's squire and page.

We know from the original documents that Joan had more good one-liners than any other figure in history. The scriptwriters for this movie made thorough use of these recorded one-liners when they gave them to Jovovich to perform. A catalog of these authentic sayings of Joan that we hear Jovovich deliver on screen follows:

- On the urgency of her mission: "Better today than tomorrow, better tomorrow than the day after."
- To her co-commanders of the army as she overrules their decisions with her strategic advice from God: "You have been with your council and I have been with mine."
- Shouting at the English commander of the Tourelles: "Glasdale! Yield to the King of Heaven! You call me a whore, but I have great pity on your soul and the souls of your men!" (Bergman delivered the same line, substituting "harlot" for "whore." I wish Sobieski's scriptwriters had given her a chance at this line.)

- As she exhorts her soldiers to follow her into battle: "Let all those who love me—follow me!"
- On the folly of Charles negotiating with the Burgundians: "We will only have peace on the point of a lance."
- To her accusers at her trial: "You say that you are my judges but take care, for you place yourselves in great danger—I am sent by God and one day you too will be judged."
- At her trial: "I loved my banner forty times more than my sword because I could never kill anyone with it. I have never killed anyone."

Hearing all these great historical utterances spilling from a movie soundtrack gladdens the heart of any scholar of Joan.

There *is* one controversial scene in the movie that does violence to the truths of history. The scene depicts Joan as a small child witnessing her elder sister being murdered and raped (in that order) by an English soldier. While the scene enables the makers of this movie to provide their version of Joan with a revenge motivation, the scene has no basis in the historical record.

The serious problem I have with this movie is Jovovich's interpretation of Joan's character. I respect Jovovich's interpretation but I cannot agree with it. Where Bergman played Joan too sweet and too nice, Jovovich errs the other way, playing her as an over-the-edge maniac. The worst example of Jovovich's histrionics is her crazed first meeting with Charles, complete with gales of heavy breathing. Still, I must concede that Jovovich's interpretation of Joan's character is consistent with, and essential to, this movie's revisionist theme.

Fortunately, Jovovich's approach works reasonably well in the battle scenes. Her overly intense performance is camouflaged by the inherent intensity of war. Her heated arguments over strategy with her co-commanders of the army (almost) play believably. When Jovovich is running wild over the battlefield, shouting her exhortations to her men and flailing about in the vortex of the fight, the mania of her performance is far more believable than Bergman's attempts at warrior excitement. (It is a shame that Sobieski's scriptwriters did not provide their Joan with such an active combat role.)

Once Jovovich is a prisoner, the excesses of her acting style again become apparent—although she does hit the right note in her saucy answers to her accusers.

Dustin Hoffman as Joan's conscience, who argues with her over the virtues and evils of how she has lived her life as she bides her final months in prison, is a bizarre touch. It is Hoffman as Joan's conscience who forces her to realize that her "divine guidance" is nothing but self-delusion driven by her hunger for revenge. Hoffman's role actually works well as an artful device of moviemaking—but it will also anger anyone in the audience who loves the traditional interpretation of Joan's life.

Appendix C

JOAN'S PERSONAL APPEARANCE

There is not enough surviving evidence to give us any certainty about what Joan looked like. There is only one surviving work of art depicting Joan that was created while she was alive. All the other thousands of portraits of her that have been drawn, painted, or sculpted, over almost six centuries, and that are still in good condition, were created after she died. The one surviving portrait of Joan made while she was alive is actually nothing but a "doodle" drawn in the margin of an official document by a clerk who worked for the pro-English Burgundian government of Paris. The clerk drew the doodle of Joan on May 10, 1429, as he was writing down the news of her breaking the siege of Orléans two days before.[1] It is inconceivable that the clerk ever actually saw Joan with his own eyes at any time before he drew his margin doodle. His little drawing can only have been based on his own imagination and on such fragmentary English reports from Orléans as had reached Paris by May 10. The doodle shows Joan with a sword and banner, and that is accurate enough. But it also shows her with long hair and wearing a dress, contradicting the two pieces of information about Joan's looks that we *do* know with virtual certainty: that her hair was cut short and that she dressed as a man. The famous Paris margin doodle cannot in any way be considered a useful piece of evidence about Joan's appearance.

Any attempt to reconstruct what Joan looked like must base itself on the few tantalizing scraps of written information left by her associates and on informed guesswork. Here follows my best effort to reconstruct Joan's appearance based on thin evidence and my own speculation.

Photo C.1 The only known surviving portrait of Joan created during her lifetime is nothing but this "doodle" drawn in the margin of an official document of the Burgundian government of Paris. The man who drew it was a bureaucrat in the service of Joan's enemies who had never seen her with his own eyes. His portrayal of her was based purely on hearsay. The sword and banner bear some relation to reality, but the long hair and dress are patently incorrect. By the time she was wielding a sword and banner, Joan sported short hair and a suit of armor. © The Art Archive / Joan of Arc birthplace Domrémy, France / Dagli Ori.

HAIR AND EYE COLOR

A government clerk of the town of La Rochelle recorded the testimony of a person who had seen Joan at Chinon to the effect that she had short black hair.[2] The great scholar Jules Quicherat, who located hundreds of pages of original period documents pertaining to Joan, made a discovery that seems to confirm that Joan had black hair. When he discovered the actual letter that Joan had sent to the people of the town of Riom, he saw a single black hair pressed into the letter's wax seal. Quicherat reported this finding in the printed collection of Joan-related documents that he published in five volumes during the 1840s. It is only reasonable to assume that the single black hair pressed into the seal of Joan's letter to the citizens of Riom was hers. Sadly for Joan enthusiasts, the single black hair and the wax seal have since been lost, even though the letter itself is still intact in the archives.[3]

Since most black-haired people have brown eyes rather than blue or green, Joan probably had brown eyes.

HEIGHT

Joan wore the clothing of Jean de Metz's male servant when she left Vaucouleurs to travel to the Dauphin at Chinon.[4] (De Metz was one of her escorts for the journey.) If the male servant was short for a man, then Joan may have been of average height for a woman. If the servant was of average height for a man, then Joan may have been tall for a woman.

BODY CONFORMATION

Two of Joan's closest companions in the field and in camp were Jean d'Aulon, her squire, and Jean, Duke of Alençon, one of her co-commanders of the army. D'Aulon saw Joan in various states of undress as he tended her wounds and helped her into and out of her armor. D'Alençon also saw Joan in various states of undress in the course of going to bed or getting up while living out of doors during their military campaigns. In his retrial testimony, d'Aulon reported he often saw her naked legs and breasts and that "she was a young girl, beautiful and well-formed." D'Alençon testified that when he sometimes looked at Joan's naked breasts, he found them "beautiful."[5] If one studies the artwork of Western Europe during the late Middle Ages and early Renaissance, one can gain an understanding of what constituted the ideal of feminine beauty for people living in that time and place. It seems evident that according to the standards of beauty prevalent in Joan's era and location, small, firm, hemispherical, high-mounted breasts were considered the most beautiful.

Joan was examined by several doctors while she was a prisoner of the English in the city of Rouen. One of these doctors, named Guillaume de la Chambre, reported that she was "stricta," that is, "narrow in the hips."[6] We know that Joan was a superb natural horse rider. This fact argues strongly for her having legs that were long and slender but excellently muscled.

Finally, we must acknowledge Joan's astonishing athleticism, strength, and endurance that her contemporaries testified about so vehemently. Regardless of her height, her body conformation must have been lean and slender but wiry and muscular. She must have been built like a world-class athlete of today in a sport such as soccer or track.

ATTRACTIVENESS

While all of Joan's military comrades swore in her retrial that they never felt sexual arousal when they were around her, knight Jean de Metz hastened to add that "I was on fire with her words, and with what I believe was her divine love." Squire Gobert Thibault elaborated on this theme when he testified that the men close to Joan *did* sometimes sexually desire her—but, as they said, they did not dare act on their desire because their love for her was a chaste love filled with awe for her saintly qualities.[7] When Joan was a prisoner, a man who held her in no such awe attempted to fondle her breasts, only to have her violently repel him.[8]

I must address this issue drawing on my twenty years of experience as a soldier in the modern, gender-integrated United States Army. Men are men and soldiers are soldiers in how they look at and how they respond to a young woman, regardless of the period of history or army in question. If Joan were ugly, she never could have commanded the chaste love and devotion that she did, no matter how much saintly purity and military skill she possessed. She may not have been a beauty of the sort to pose for the cover of *Vogue* magazine—but, at least, she *must* have been attractive in a fresh, healthy, girl-next-door sort of way for all her men to respond to her as they did. It was her approachable good looks *in combination with* her pure heart, her keen mind, her athletic ability, and her raw courage that *compelled* her companions to respect her as their warrior equal and to chastely love her as their Pucelle.

CONCLUSION

The picture we now have of Joan is a young woman with short, black hair, brown eyes, more or less average height, a slender but superbly healthy, athletic build, and a bright, approachable, love-commanding attractiveness. I see a teenage version of Mia Hamm, the great American soccer player, with her hair cut short.

NOTES

CHAPTER 1: THE TWO KEY QUESTIONS ABOUT JOAN OF ARC'S MILITARY CAREER: "WHAT" AND "HOW"

1. It is a useful device to begin a work on Joan by listing all the various ways that different people with different agendas have chosen to view her over the centuries. Though our lists are different, Kelly DeVries uses this technique to good effect to open his essay, "A Woman as Leader of Men: Joan of Arc's Military Career," in *Fresh Verdicts on Joan of Arc,* ed. Bonnie Wheeler and Charles T. Wood (New York: Garland Publishing, 1996), 3.

2. A summary of Joan's career can be distilled from any of the dozens of available biographies of her. Three of the most useful are: V. Sackville-West, *Saint Joan of Arc,* rev. ed. (London: Michael Joseph, 1948); Frances Gies, *Joan of Arc: The Legend and the Reality* (New York: Harper & Row, 1981); and Edward A. Lucie-Smith, *Joan of Arc* (New York: W. W. Norton, 1977). It is necessary to enter the caveat that Lucie-Smith's work must be used with some caution. His book is an example of psychological biography and contains several paragraphs of what some may disparage as pointless attempts to analyze Joan's thoughts and feelings, both conscious and subconscious. When he sticks to straight historical narrative, which he does most of the time, he does a respectable job. Like many peasants of her time and place, Joan was unsure as to her own exact age. At her trial for heresy, she stated that she thought her age was about nineteen, which would have made her about seventeen at the time of her greatest military and political feats. This also would have put the year of her birth at about 1412. See Pierre Tisset and Yvonne Lanhers, eds. and trans., *Procès de condemnation de Jeanne d'Arc,* 3 vols. (Paris: Klincksieck, 1960–71), 2:41.

3. Edouard Perroy, *The Hundred Years War,* trans. W.B. Wells (New York: Capricorn Books, 1965), 283.

4. Gies, *Joan of Arc: The Legend and the Reality,* 83–88.

5. Colonel Ferdinand de Liocourt, *La mission de Jeanne d'Arc* (Paris: Nouvelles Éditions Latines, 1974), vol. 1, *Le plan d'action,* 1:360–363; and vol. 2, *L'exécution,* 2:114.

6. Lieutenant-Colonel de Lancesseur, *Jeanne d'Arc, Chef de Guerre: Le génie militaire et politique de Jeanne d'Arc, Campagne de France 1429–1430* (Paris: Nouvelles Éditions Debresse, 1961), 137.

CHAPTER 2: THE STORY OF JOAN'S STORY: A REVIEW OF THE LITERATURE

1. Régine Pernoud and Marie-Véronique Clin, *Joan of Arc: Her Story,* trans. and rev. Jeremy du Quesnay Adams (New York: St. Martin's Press, 1998), 139, 157.

2. Jules Quicherat, ed., *Procès de condemnation et de réhabilitation de Jeanne d'Arc dite la Pucelle,* 5 vols. (Paris: Chez Jules Renouard et Cie, 1841–49; reprint, New York: Johnson Reprint Corp., 1965) (the reprint is an exact facsimile of the original, thus preserving the original pagination).

3. Pierre Tisset and Yvonne Lanhers, eds. and trans., *Procès de condemnation de Jeanne d'Arc,* 3 vols. (Paris: Klincksieck, 1960–71).

4. Pierre Duparc, ed., *Procès en nullité de la condemnation de Jeanne d'Arc,* 5 vols. (Paris: Klincksieck, 1977–89).

5. Nadia Margolis, *Joan of Arc in History, Literature, and Film* (New York: Garland Publishing, 1990). A capsule biography of Margolis is in Bonnie Wheeler and Charles T. Wood, eds., *Fresh Verdicts on Joan of Arc* (New York: Garland Publishing, 1996), 316.

6. Jules Michelet, "Jeanne d'Arc," in *Oeuvres Complètes: Etude du ms. et examen des remaniements du texte de 1841 et 1844 à travers les rééditions par Robert Casanova*, vol. 6, ed. Paul Viallaneix (Paris: Flammarion, 1978), 6:60–122; and Margolis, *Joan of Arc in History,* 128–29.

7. Mark Twain, *Personal Recollections of Joan of Arc* (New York: Harper's, 1896); and Margolis, *Joan of Arc in History,* 326.

8. Anatole France, *Vie de Jeanne d'Arc,* 2 vols. (Paris: Calmann-Lévy, 1908); and Margolis, *Joan of Arc in History,* 119–20.

9. Andrew Lang, *The Maid of France: Being the Story of the Life and Death of Jeanne d'Arc* (London: Longman's, 1908); and Margolis, *Joan of Arc in History,* 125–26.

10. V. Sackville-West, *Saint Joan of Arc,* rev. ed. (London: Michael Joseph, 1948); Margolis, *Joan of Arc in History,* 132–33.

11. Frances Gies, *Joan of Arc: The Legend and the Reality* (New York: Harper & Row, 1981); Margolis, *Joan of Arc in History,* 150.

12. Edward A. Lucie-Smith, *Joan of Arc* (New York: W.W. Norton, 1977); Margolis, *Joan of Arc in History,* 127.

13. Régine Pernoud, *Joan of Arc by Herself and Her Witnesses,* trans. Edward Hyams (N.p.: Stein and Day, 1966; reprint, New York: Scarborough House, 1994) (page citations are to the reprint edition); Régine Pernoud, *The Retrial of Joan of Arc: The Evidence at the Trial for Her Rehabilitation, 1450–1456,* trans. J.M. Cohen, with a foreword by Katherine Anne Porter (New York: Harcourt, Brace and Co., 1955); and Margolis, *Joan of Arc in History,* 25, 131.

14. Marina Warner, *Joan of Arc: The Image of Female Heroism* (London: Weidenfeld and Nicolson, 1981); and Margolis, *Joan of Arc in History,* 154.

15. Karen Sullivan, *The Interrogation of Joan of Arc* (Minneapolis: University of Minnesota Press, 1999); and Deborah A. Fraioli, *Joan of Arc: The Early Debate* (Woodbridge, England: Boydell Press, 2000).

16. Michel de Lombarès, "Patay 18 Juin 1429," *Revue historique de l'armée* 22 (1966): 5–16; and Margolis, *Joan of Arc in History,* 185.

17. Philippe Contamine, *War in the Middle Ages,* trans. Michael Jones (New York: Barnes and Noble, 1998); Contamine, "Les armées française et anglaise a l'époque de Jeanne d'Arc," *Revue des sociétés savantes de haute normandie* 57 (1970): 5–33; and Contamine, "La guerre de siège au temps de Jeanne d'Arc," *Dossiers de archéologie* 34 (May 1979): 11–20.

18. Kelly DeVries, "A Woman as Leader of Men: Joan of Arc's Military Career," in *Fresh Verdicts on Joan of Arc,* ed. Bonnie Wheeler and Charles T. Wood (New York: Garland Publishing, 1996), 3–18. See also DeVries's book *Joan of Arc: A Military Leader* (Gloustershire, England: Sutton Publishing, 1999); and his "The Use of Gunpowder Weaponry by and against Joan of Arc during the Hundred Years War," *War and Society* 14 (May 1996): 1–15.

CHAPTER 3: THE GENERAL SITUATION PRIOR TO JOAN'S ARRIVAL ON THE PUBLIC STAGE

1. For a thorough discussion of the religiosity of late medieval western Europe, see Norman F. Cantor, *The Civilization of the Middle Ages* (New York: HarperCollins, 1993; reprint, HarperPerennial, 1994), 373–93, 417–48, 483, 487–505, and 519. Aron Gurevich points out the extreme literal-mindedness of medieval religious belief with regard to direct divine intervention in worldly affairs in his *Medieval Popular Culture: Problems of Belief and Perception,* trans. János M. Bak and Paul A. Hollingsworth (Cambridge: Cambridge University Press, 1988; reprint, Cambridge: Cambridge University Press, 1997), 45, 54, 65, and 77 (page citations are to the reprint edition). See also Christopher Allmand, ed., *Society at War: The Experience of England and France during the Hundred Years War* (Edinburgh: Oliver and Boyd, 1973; reprint, Woodbridge, England: Boydell Press, 1998), 40–43, for specific discussion of God's perceived role in the medieval mind in determining the outcomes of battles and wars (page citations are to the reprint edition).

2. Edward A. Lucie-Smith, *Joan of Arc* (New York: W. W. Norton, 1977), 69. Norman F. Cantor, *The Civilization of the Middle Ages* (New York: HarperCollins, 1993; reprint, HarperPerennial, 1994), 519, specifically describes Joan's mysticism in the context of the Hundred Years' War.

3. Cantor, *Civilization of the Middle Ages,* 472–76. See Nicholas Wright, *Knights and Peasants: The Hundred Years War in the French Countryside* (Woodbridge, England: Boydell Press, 1998), 96–116, for a detailed discussion of the communal self-defense measures taken by peasants on their own initiative during the Hundred Years' War.

4. The following discussion of the changes in the conduct of war during the Hundred Years' War, and of the resistance of chivalrous nobles to these changes, is summarized from Carl Stephenson, *Medieval Feudalism* (Ithaca, N.Y.: Cornell University Press, 1942; reprint, Cornell Paperbacks, 1965), 27–29, 102–4; Cantor, *Civilization of the Middle Ages,* 465–68, 484–86; Phillipe Contamine, *War in the Middle Ages,* trans. Michael Jones (New York: Barnes and Noble, 1998), 150–72; Allmand, *Society at War,* 5, 44; and Major-General J.F.C. Fuller, *A Military History of the Western World: From the Earliest Times to the Battle of Lepanto* (New York: Funk and Wagnalls, 1954), 441–42, 449. The standard of forty days of obligatory feudal military service per year was subject to local variation.

5. Philippe Contamine, "Les armées française et anglaise a l'époque de Jeanne d'Arc," *Revue des sociétés savantes de haute normandie* 57 (1970): 16–17; and Jules Quicherat, ed., *Procès de condemnation et de réhabilitation de Jeanne d'Arc dite la Pucelle,* 5 vols. (Paris: Chez Jules Renouard et Cie, 1841–49; reprint, New York: Johnson Reprint Corp., 1965), 4:18.

6. Stephenson, *Medieval Feudalism,* 66–68; Charles Oman, *The Art of War in the Middle Ages, A.D. 378–1515,* rev. and ed. John H. Beeler (Ithaca, N.Y.: Cornell University Press, 1953; reprint, Cornell Paperbacks, 1968), 57–62, 124–25; Johan Huizinga, "The Political and Military Significance of Chivalric Ideas in the Late Middle Ages," in *Men and Ideas, History, the Middle Ages, the Renaissance: Essays by Johan Huizinga,* trans. James S. Holmes and Hans van Marle (New York: Meridian Books, 1959), 199–200, 202–3; also see Charity Cannon Willard's introduction to Christine de Pizan's *The Book of Deeds of Arms and of Chivalry,* trans. Sumner Willard, ed. Charity Cannon Willard (University Park, Pa.: Pennsylvania State University Press, 1999), 3, 5; and Fuller, *A Military History of the Western World,* 449.

7. Richard W. Kaeuper and Elspeth Kennedy, *The Book of Chivalry of Geoffroi de Charny: Text, Context, and Translation* (Philadelphia: University of Pennsylvania Press, 1996.)

8. Ibid., 103–7.

9. Ibid., 3–18.

10. The following summary of the Hundred Years' War up until the advent of Joan is derived from Lieutenant-Colonel Alfred H. Burne, *The Crécy War: A Military History of the Hundred Years War from 1337 to the Peace of Bretigny, 1360*

(N.p.: Eyre and Spottiswoode, 1955; reprint, Ware, England: Wordsworth, 1999); and his *The Agincourt War: A Military History of the Latter Part of the Hundred Years War from 1369 to 1453* (N.p.: Eyre and Spottiswoode, 1956; reprint, Ware, England: Wordsworth, 1999), 17–236 (page citations are to the reprint edition); and Fuller, *A Military History of the Western World*, 441–80. A reference work useful for establishing the basic chronology of this period is R. Earnest Dupuy and Trevor N. Dupuy, *The Harper Encyclopedia of Military History*, 4th ed. (New York: Harper Collins, 1993), 382–89, 444–51.

11. Stephenson, *Medieval Feudalism*, 66–68; Oman, *The Art of War*, 57–62, 124–25; Huizinga, "The Political and Military Significance of Chivalric Ideas," 199–200, 202–3; and Willard's introduction to de Pizan, *The Book of Deeds*, 3, 5.

12. B. H. Liddell Hart, *Strategy*, 2d ed. (New York: Signet, 1974), 59; Charles Oman, *A History of the Art of War in the Middle Ages*, vol. 2, *1278–1485*, 2nd ed. (London: Methuen and Co., 1924), 196–202; and Régine Pernoud and Marie-Véronique Clin, *Joan of Arc: Her Story*, trans. and rev. Jeremy du Quesnay Adams (New York: St. Martin's Press, 1998), 179–80.

13. The following narrative of the Battle of Agincourt is derived from John Keegan, *The Face of Battle* (New York: Viking, 1976), 79–116. Among readers of military history, Keegan's narrative of Agincourt is considered a classic of descriptive prose. However, Keegan's fame as a writer of military history rests on his skill as a synthesizer of secondary sources, not on any original research he has done in primary sources. Keegan's bibliography in his *Face of Battle* lists no primary sources in the section for Agincourt. Alfred H. Burne, on pages 94–96 of his *Agincourt War*, cites three of the key primary-source documents for Agincourt as the *Henrici Quinti Angliae regis gesta*, the *Vita et gesta Henrici quinti*, and the *Vita Henrici Quinti*. Burne also cites the importance of the contemporary accounts of the battle written by Enguerrand Monstrelet, Le Fèvre, Lord of St. Remy, Jean de Wavrin, and the Monk of Saint Denys.

14. Christopher Rothero, *The Armies of Agincourt* (London: Osprey, 1981), 24–26.

15. Eyewitness account of Jean de Wavrin, quoted in Allmand, *Society at War*, 107.

16. Rothero, *Armies of Agincourt*, plate A, fig. 2; and 33.

17. Fuller, *A Military History of the Western World*, 457.

18. Stephenson, *Medieval Feudalism*, 66–68; Oman, *The Art of War*, 57–62, 124–25; Huizinga, "The Political and Military Significance of Chivalric Ideas," 199–200, 202–3; and Willard's introduction to de Pizan, *The Book of Deeds*, 3, 5.

19. Keegan, *The Face of Battle*, 83 (map).

20. Ibid., 89.

21. Ibid., 84–86, 90–107.

22. Burne, *Agincourt War*, 87, 90–91, 93.

23. The following summary of the Hundred Years' War from Agincourt to the coming of Joan is derived from Burne, *Agincourt War*, 97–236; Fuller, *A Military*

History of the Western World, 475–80; and Dupuy and Dupuy, *Harper Encyclopedia of Military History,* 450–51.

24. Dupuy and Dupuy, *Harper Encyclopedia of Military History,* 452.

CHAPTER 4: JOAN'S MILITARY CAREER: THE PRELIMINARIES

1. The following narrative of Joan's early life and ascent to a position of influence is summarized from V. Sackville-West, *Saint Joan of Arc,* rev. ed. (London: Michael Joseph, 1948), 30–134; Frances Gies, *Joan of Arc: The Legend and the Reality* (New York: Harper & Row, 1981), 6–61; and Edward A. Lucie-Smith, *Joan of Arc* (New York: W.W. Norton, 1977), 11–38, 51–89. Sackville-West provides a minutely detailed chronology of Joan's life that tracks all her travels on a day-to-day basis. This chronology, on 331–33 of the revised edition of Sackville-West's book, is a godsend for the student of Joan. However, there is one irritating discrepancy in Sackville-West's chronology. The chronology says that Joan left Blois for Orléans on April 25, 1429, contradicting Sackville-West's own main text, which gives this date as April 27 (142). Gies, *Joan of Arc: The Legend,* 61, and Lucie-Smith, *Joan of Arc,* 89, both give the date as the 27th. The 27th is the date that I have used.

2. Sackville-West, *Saint Joan of Arc,* 32–35; and Régine Pernoud and Marie-Véronique Clin, *Joan of Arc: Her Story,* trans. and rev. Jeremy du Quesnay Adams (New York: St. Martin's Press, 1998), 221–22.

3. Gies, *Joan of Arc: The Legend,* 10.

4. Pierre Tisset and Yvonne Lanhers, eds. and trans., *Procès de condemnation de Jeanne d'Arc,* 3 vols. (Paris: Klincksieck, 1960–71), 2:41.

5. Ibid., 2:64–65.

6. Sackville-West, *Saint Joan of Arc,* 72–74.

7. Tisset and Lanhers, *Procès de condemnation de Jeanne d'Arc,* 2:46–48, 71–73, 88, 113, 136–37; and Pierre Duparc, ed., *Procès en nullité de la condemnation de Jeanne d'Arc,* 5 vols. (Paris: Klincksieck, 1977–89), 4:8.

8. Tisset and Lanhers, *Procès de condemnation de Jeanne d'Arc,* 2:47–48.

9. Sackville-West, *Saint Joan of Arc,* 68.

10. Duparc, *Procès en nullité de la condemnation,* 3:283.

11. Ibid., 2:283, 292–93. See also Jules Quicherat, ed., *Procès de condemnation et de réhabilitation de Jeanne d'Arc dite la Pucelle,* 5 vols. (Paris: Chez Jules Renouard et Cie, 1841–49; reprint, New York: Johnson Reprint Corp., 1965), 4:205; Sackville-West, *Saint Joan of Arc,* 70–71; and Gies, *Joan of Arc: The Legend,* 32.

12. Sackville-West, *Saint Joan of Arc,* 77–80.

13. Duparc, *Procès en nullité de la condemnation,* 3:277; Sackville-West, *Saint Joan of Arc,* 85; and Lucie-Smith, *Joan of Arc,* 30–31.

14. Gies, *Joan of Arc: The Legend,* 36; and Lucie-Smith, *Joan of Arc,* 31, 37.

15. Quicherat, *Procès de condemnation et de réhabilitation,* 4:125, 206, 208; Sackville-West, *Saint Joan of Arc,* 98, 329; and Gies, *Joan of Arc: The Legend,* 36.

16. Duparc, *Procès en nullité de la condemnation,* 3:285; and Sackville-West, *Saint Joan of Arc,* 88–90.

17. Duparc, *Procès en nullité de la condemnation,* 3:278, 293; Gies, *Joan of Arc: The Legend,* 36; and Lucie-Smith, *Joan of Arc,* 37.

18. Duparc, *Procès en nullité de la condemnation,* 3:277, 293; and Sackville-West, *Saint Joan of Arc,* 98–99.

19. Tisset and Lanhers, *Procès de condemnation de Jeanne d'Arc,* 2:48; Duparc, *Procès en nullité de la condemnation,* 3:277–78, 293, and 4:47, 62, 64; Quicherat, *Procès de condemnation et de réhabilitation,* 5:107; Sackville-West, *Saint Joan of Arc,* 99, 119–20; and Lucie-Smith, *Joan of Arc,* 31–32.

20. Tisset and Lanhers, *Procès de condemnation de Jeanne d'Arc,* 2:52, 54; Sackville-West, *Saint Joan of Arc,* 100, 331; Gies, *Joan of Arc: The Legend,* 36; and Lucie-Smith, *Joan of Arc,* 38. Sackville-West says that Joan left Vaucouleurs on February 23, 1429. Gies and Lucie-Smith say she left on February 13.

21. Duparc, *Procès en nullité de la condemnation,* 3:278, 293; Sackville-West, *Saint Joan of Arc,* 100, 102–6; Gies, *Joan of Arc: The Legend,* 37; and Lucie-Smith, *Joan of Arc,* 51–56. Sackville-West says Joan arrived at Chinon on March 6. Lucie-Smith says she arrived on February 23, while Gies says she arrived eleven days after leaving Vaucouleurs.

22. Duparc, *Procès en nullité de la condemnation,* 4:2–3; Sackville-West, *Saint Joan of Arc,* 101, 127–28; Gies, *Joan of Arc: The Legend,* 44; and Lucie-Smith, *Joan of Arc,* 53–54.

23. Duparc, *Procès en nullité de la condemnation,* 4:81–82; Gies, *Joan of Arc: The Legend,* 46–49; and Lucie-Smith, *Joan of Arc,* 55–56.

24. Duparc, *Procès en nullité de la condemnation,* 4:11, 72, 82, 141; Quicherat, *Procès de condemnation et de réhabilitation,* 4:52–53; Sackville-West, *Saint Joan of Arc,* 112–13; Gies, *Joan of Arc: The Legend,* 49–50; and Lucie-Smith, *Joan of Arc,* 58.

25. Sackville-West, *Saint Joan of Arc,* 107–8, 328; and Lucie-Smith, *Joan of Arc,* 58–59. See also the famous and almost brutally frank portrait of Charles painted from life by Jean Fouquet (photo, chap. 4).

26. Duparc, *Procès en nullité de la condemnation,* 4:72, 82; Sackville-West, *Saint Joan of Arc,* 113–17; Gies, *Joan of Arc: The Legend,* 50–52; and Lucie-Smith, *Joan of Arc,* 59–69.

27. Sackville-West, *Saint Joan of Arc,* 120; Gies, *Joan of Arc: The Legend,* 52; and Lucie-Smith, *Joan of Arc,* 69.

28. Duparc, *Procès en nullité de la condemnation,* 4:64; and Sackville-West, *Saint Joan of Arc,* 118–19.

29. Gies, *Joan of Arc: The Legend,* 53.

30. Duparc, *Procès en nullité de la condemnation,* 4:149–52; Sackville-West, *Saint Joan of Arc,* 124–26; and Gies, *Joan of Arc: The Legend,* 53–56.

31. Duparc, *Procès en nullité de la condemnation,* 4:71; and Sackville-West, *Saint Joan of Arc,* 120, 126–27.

32. Quicherat, *Procès de condemnation et de réhabilitation,* 5:95–98; Pernoud and Clin, *Joan of Arc: Her Story,* 33–34, 249–50; Lucie-Smith, *Joan of Arc,* 78–79; and Willard Trask, ed. and trans., *Joan of Arc in Her Own Words* (New York: Turtle Point Press, 1996), 28–30.

33. Sackville-West, *Saint Joan of Arc,* 129–30, 155.

34. Quicherat, *Procès de condemnation et de réhabilitation,* 4:425–28; Sackville-West, *Saint Joan of Arc,* 151, 329–30; and Lucie-Smith, *Joan of Arc,* 118.

35. Gies, *Joan of Arc: The Legend,* 59–60; and Pernoud and Clin, 224–25.

36. Gies, *Joan of Arc: The Legend,* 57.

37. Ibid., 60.

38. Ibid., 61; and Lieutenant-Colonel Alfred H. Burne, *The Agincourt War: A Military History of the Latter Part of the Hundred Years War from 1369 to 1453* (N.p.: Eyre and Spottiswoode, 1956; reprint, Ware, England: Wordsworth, 1999), 237.

39. Duparc, *Procès en nullité de la condemnation,* 4:65–66; Gies, *Joan of Arc: The Legend,* 61; and Lucie-Smith, *Joan of Arc,* 88.

CHAPTER 5: JOAN'S ACHIEVEMENT IN RAISING FRENCH MORALE: THE FIRST PART OF "WHAT"

1. Pierre Duparc, ed., *Procès en nullité de la condemnation de Jeanne d'Arc,* 5 vols. (Paris: Klincksieck, 1977–89), 1:473–88; 3:276–79, 291–94; and 4:2–11, 46–51, 64–79; and Régine Pernoud and Marie-Véronique Clin, *Joan of Arc: Her Story,* trans. and rev. Jeremy du Quesnay Adams (New York: St. Martin's Press, 1998), 180–81.

2. Duparc, *Procès en nullité de la condemnation,* 4:5.

3. Nadia Margolis, *Joan of Arc in History, Literature, and Film* (New York: Garland Publishing, 1990), 69–70.

4. Jules Quicherat, ed., *Procès de condemnation et de réhabilitation de Jeanne d'Arc dite la Pucelle,* 5 vols. (Paris: Chez Jules Renouard et Cie, 1841–49; reprint, New York: Johnson Reprint Corp., 1965), 4:418.

5. Régine Pernoud, *Joan of Arc by Herself and Her Witnesses,* trans. Edward Hyams (N.p.: Stein and Day, 1966; reprint, New York: Scarborough House, 1994) (page citations are to the reprint edition), 100; Régine Pernoud, *The Retrial of Joan of Arc: The Evidence at the Trial for Her Rehabilitation, 1450–1456,* trans. J.M. Cohen, with a foreword by Katherine Anne Porter (New York: Harcourt, Brace and Co., 1955), 118; and Quicherat, *Procès de condemnation et de réhabilitation,* 5:162–64, 192–94. The duke of Gloucester's two edicts are dated May 3

and December 12, 1430. The date on the second document shows that the English were afraid of Joan even after she had been captured!

6. Quicherat, *Procès de condemnation et de réhabilitation,* 5:136–37; and Lieutenant-Colonel Alfred H. Burne, *The Agincourt War: A Military History of the Latter Part of the Hundred Years War from 1369 to 1453* (N.p.: Eyre and Spottiswoode, 1956; reprint, Ware, England: Wordsworth, 1999), 266–67.

7. Duparc, *Procès en nullité de la condemnation,* 4:15, 25, 51, 54–55, 57, 69–70, 73, 75, 85, 152; V. Sackville-West, *Saint Joan of Arc,* rev. ed. (London: Michael Joseph, 1948), 143; Frances Gies, *Joan of Arc: The Legend and the Reality* (New York: Harper & Row, 1981), 61; and Edward A. Lucie-Smith, *Joan of Arc* (New York: W. W. Norton, 1977), 97.

8. George Bernard Shaw, *Saint Joan* (New York: Brentano's, 1924), xxxiii–xxxiv.

9. Duparc, *Procès en nullité de la condemnation,* 4:57.

10. Jane Marie Pinzino, "Just War, Joan of Arc and the Politics of Salvation," unpublished manuscript (Tacoma, Wash.: University of Puget Sound, 2001).

11. Giovanni da Legnano, *Tractatus de Bello, de Represaliis et de Duello* [Tractate on War, Reprisals, and the Duel], trans. James Leslie Brierly and ed. Thomas Erskine Holland (Oxford: Oxford University Press, 1917); and Honoré Bonet, *Arbre des Batailles* [The Tree of Battles], trans. G. W. Coopland (Cambridge, Mass.: Harvard University Press, 1949).

12. Pinzino, "Just War," 11–12.

13. Da Legnano, *Tractatus de Bello,* 235–37; and Bonet, *Arbre des Batailles,* 130–32.

14. Duparc, *Procès en nullité de la condemnation,* 1:480–82.

15. Pernoud, *Retrial of Joan of Arc,* 120.

16. Duparc, *Procès en nullité de la condemnation,* 4:66–68.

17. Pierre Tisset and Yvonne Lanhers, eds. and trans., *Procès de condemnation de Jeanne d'Arc,* 3 vols. (Paris: Klincksieck, 1960–71), 2:79.

18. Quicherat, *Procès de condemnation et de réhabilitation,* 4:446.

19. Duparc, *Procès en nullité de la condemnation,* 1:484; and 4:6, 49, 77.

20. Duparc, *Procès en nullité de la condemnation,* 4:68.

21. Quicherat, *Procès de condemnation et de réhabilitation,* 4:27.

22. Duparc, *Procès en nullité de la condemnation,* 4:6.

23. Ibid., 4:50.

24. Ibid., 4:16, 57, 59, 61; Tisset and Lanhers, *Procès de condemnation de Jeanne d'Arc,* 2:96–97; and Quicherat, *Procès de condemnation et de réhabilitation,* 4:153.

25. Gies, *Joan of Arc: The Legend* 90; and Kelly DeVries, *Joan of Arc: A Military Leader* (Gloustershire, England: Sutton Publishing, 1999), 108.

26. Quicherat, *Procès de condemnation et de réhabilitation,* 4:18. See also Philippe Contamine, "Les armées française et anglaise a l'époque de Jeanne d'Arc," *Revue des sociétés savantes de haute normandie* 57 (1970): 16–17, for a

quick discussion of Charles's military recruiting problems before the coming of Joan. Contamine cites the "general lassitude" as well as the poor financial situation and the fact that many nobles declined to fight for Charles.

27. Quicherat, *Procès de condemnation et de réhabilitation,* 5:108–9.

28. Lucie-Smith, *Joan of Arc,* 129.

CHAPTER 6: JOAN'S ACHIEVEMENT AS A MILITARY COMMANDER: THE SECOND PART OF "WHAT"

1. Frances Gies, *Joan of Arc: The Legend and the Reality* (New York: Harper & Row, 1981), 85.

2. Pierre Duparc, ed., *Procès en nullité de la condemnation de Jeanne d'Arc,* 5 vols. (Paris: Klincksieck, 1977–89), 4:82.

3. Ibid., 4:86.

4. Ibid., 4:70.

5. V. Sackville-West, *Saint Joan of Arc,* rev. ed. (London: Michael Joseph, 1948), 139; and Lieutenant-Colonel Alfred H. Burne, *The Agincourt War: A Military History of the Latter Part of the Hundred Years War from 1369 to 1453* (N.p.: Eyre and Spottiswoode, 1956; reprint, Ware, England: Wordsworth, 1999), 229.

6. Burne, *Agincourt War,* 229.

7. Régine Pernoud and Marie-Véronique Clin, *Joan of Arc: Her Story,* trans. and rev. Jeremy du Quesnay Adams (New York: St. Martin's Press, 1998), 226–30.

8. Burne, *Agincourt War,* 228–29.

9. David Nicolle, *Orléans 1429 France Turns the Tide* (Oxford: Osprey Publishing, 2001), 35.

10. Burne, *Agincourt War,* 229, 233–34.

11. Ibid., 234.

12. Gies, *Joan of Arc: The Legend,* 61; and Burne, *Agincourt War,* 237.

13. Burne, *Agincourt War,* 238; Sackville-West, *Saint Joan of Arc,* 145–47; and Gies, *Joan of Arc: The Legend,* 70–71.

14. Duparc, *Procès en nullité de la condemnation,* 4:48; Sackville-West, *Saint Joan of Arc,* 144; Gies, *Joan of Arc: The Legend,* 70; and Edward A. Lucie-Smith, *Joan of Arc* (New York: W.W. Norton, 1977), 99.

15. Sackville-West, *Saint Joan of Arc,* 144–47; Gies, *Joan of Arc: The Legend,* 71; and Lucie-Smith, *Joan of Arc,* 99.

16. Duparc, *Procès en nullité de la condemnation,* 4:2–4; Sackville-West, *Saint Joan of Arc,* 145–46; Gies, *Joan of Arc: The Legend,* 71; and Lucie-Smith, *Joan of Arc,* 100–101.

17. The general narrative of Joan's actions at Orléans is well known and has been repeated dozens of times. The account that follows is summarized from the testimony of witnesses at Joan's posthumous retrial, as edited by Duparc, and from the period chronicles, as collected and edited by Quicherat. See also

Sackville-West, *Saint Joan of Arc,* 142–78; Gies, *Joan of Arc: The Legend,* 62–82; and Lucie-Smith, *Joan of Arc,* 98–125.

18. Duparc, *Procès en nullité de la condemnation,* 4:4; Sackville-West, *Saint Joan of Arc,* 145–46; Gies, *Joan of Arc: The Legend,* 71; and Lucie-Smith, *Joan of Arc,* 99.

19. Duparc, *Procès en nullité de la condemnation,* 4:4–5, 74; Sackville-West, *Saint Joan of Arc,* 147–48; Gies, *Joan of Arc: The Legend,* 71–72; and Lucie-Smith, *Joan of Arc,* 100–1.

20. Jules Quicherat, ed., *Procès de condemnation et de réhabilitation de Jeanne d'Arc dite la Pucelle,* 5 vols. (Paris: Chez Jules Renouard et Cie, 1841–49; reprint, New York: Johnson Reprint Corp., 1965), 4:218; Duparc, *Procès en nullité de la condemnation,* 4:4–5, 12; Sackville-West, *Saint Joan of Arc,* 147; Gies, *Joan of Arc: The Legend,* 71; and Lucie-Smith, *Joan of Arc,* 100.

21. Quicherat, *Procès de condemnation et de réhabilitation,* 4:151–52; Sackville-West, *Saint Joan of Arc,* 147; Gies, *Joan of Arc: The Legend,* 71; and Lucie-Smith, *Joan of Arc,* 100.

22. Quicherat, *Procès de condemnation et de réhabilitation,* 4:152; and Sackville-West, *Saint Joan of Arc,* 148–49.

23. Quicherat, *Procès de condemnation et de réhabilitation,* 4:153.

24. Ibid., 4:152–53, 219–20; Duparc, *Procès en nullité de la condemnation,* 4:48; Sackville-West, *Saint Joan of Arc,* 149–50; Gies, *Joan of Arc: The Legend,* 72; and Lucie-Smith, *Joan of Arc,* 101–2.

25. Duparc, *Procès en nullité de la condemnation,* 4:48; Quicherat, *Procès de condemnation et de réhabilitation,* 4:154; Sackville-West, *Saint Joan of Arc,* 153–54; Gies, *Joan of Arc: The Legend,* 72; and Lucie-Smith, *Joan of Arc,* 103.

26. Duparc, *Procès en nullité de la condemnation,* 4:5, 18, 90; Sackville-West, *Saint Joan of Arc,* 129–30, 155–56; Gies, *Joan of Arc: The Legend,* 72; and Lucie-Smith, *Joan of Arc,* 103–4.

27. Quicherat, *Procès de condemnation et de réhabilitation,* 4:154–55; Duparc, *Procès en nullité de la condemnation,* 4:48; Sackville-West, *Saint Joan of Arc,* 156; Gies, *Joan of Arc: The Legend,* 73; and Lucie-Smith, *Joan of Arc,* 104–5.

28. Duparc, *Procès en nullité de la condemnation,* 1:478; Quicherat, *Procès de condemnation et de réhabilitation,* 4:155–56; Sackville-West, *Saint Joan of Arc,* 156–58; Gies, *Joan of Arc: The Legend,* 73; and Lucie-Smith, *Joan of Arc,* 105.

29. Quicherat, *Procès de condemnation et de réhabilitation,* 4:156; Sackville-West, *Saint Joan of Arc,* 158; Gies, *Joan of Arc: The Legend,* 73–74; and Lucie-Smith, *Joan of Arc,* 105.

30. Quicherat, *Procès de condemnation et de réhabilitation,* 4:222; Sackville-West, *Saint Joan of Arc,* 158; and Lucie-Smith, *Joan of Arc,* 106.

31. Quicherat, *Procès de condemnation et de réhabilitation,* 4:156–57; Duparc, *Procès en nullité de la condemnation,* 4:74; Sackville-West, *Saint Joan of Arc,* 158–59; Gies, *Joan of Arc: The Legend,* 74; and Lucie-Smith, *Joan of Arc,* 106.

32. Duparc, *Procès en nullité de la condemnation*, 1:478–79; Sackville-West, *Saint Joan of Arc*, 159–60; Gies, *Joan of Arc: The Legend*, 74; and Lucie-Smith, *Joan of Arc*, 106.

33. Duparc, *Procès en nullité de la condemnation*, 1:479; 4:48, 74; Sackville-West, *Saint Joan of Arc*, 160–61; Gies, *Joan of Arc: The Legend*, 74–75; and Lucie-Smith, *Joan of Arc*, 106–7.

34. Duparc, *Procès en nullité de la condemnation*, 4:89.

35. Duparc, *Procès en nullité de la condemnation*, 1:479.

36. Duparc, *Procès en nullité de la condemnation*, 1:479–80; 4:48–49, 74–75; Quicherat, *Procès de condemnation et de réhabilitation*, 4:157–58; Sackville-West, *Saint Joan of Arc*, 161–63; Gies, *Joan of Arc: The Legend*, 75; and Lucie-Smith, *Joan of Arc*, 107–8.

37. Duparc, *Procès en nullité de la condemnation*, 4:75; Sackville-West, *Saint Joan of Arc*, 163; Gies, *Joan of Arc: The Legend*, 75; and Lucie-Smith, *Joan of Arc*, 109.

38. Quicherat, *Procès de condemnation et de réhabilitation*, 4:57–60; Sackville-West, *Saint Joan of Arc*, 163–65; Gies, *Joan of Arc: The Legend*, 75–76; and Lucie-Smith, *Joan of Arc*, 109–10.

39. Duparc, *Procès en nullité de la condemnation*, 4:75–76; Sackville-West, *Saint Joan of Arc*, 165; and Pernoud and Clin, *Joan of Arc: Her Story*, 44–45.

40. Duparc, *Procès en nullité de la condemnation*, 4:76; Sackville-West, *Saint Joan of Arc*, 165; Gies, *Joan of Arc: The Legend*, 76; and Lucie-Smith, *Joan of Arc*, 111.

41. Duparc, *Procès en nullité de la condemnation*, 1:480–82, 4:49; Quicherat, *Procès de condemnation et de réhabilitation*, 4:227; Sackville-West, *Saint Joan of Arc*, 165–67; Gies, *Joan of Arc: The Legend*, 76–78; and Lucie-Smith, *Joan of Arc*, 111–14.

42. Duparc, *Procès en nullité de la condemnation*, 4:76–77; Sackville-West, *Saint Joan of Arc*, 167; Gies, *Joan of Arc: The Legend*, 78; and Lucie-Smith, *Joan of Arc*, 114–15.

43. Quicherat, *Procès de condemnation et de réhabilitation*, 4:227, 5:293; Gies, *Joan of Arc: The Legend*, 78; and Lucie-Smith, *Joan of Arc*, 115.

44. Duparc, *Procès en nullité de la condemnation*, 4:77; Quicherat, *Procès de condemnation et de réhabilitation*, 5:293; and Lucie-Smith, *Joan of Arc*, 116.

45. Duparc, *Procès en nullité de la condemnation*, 4:82–83. Gies, *Joan of Arc: The Legend*, 78–79, relates the incident with de Gaucourt; Sackville-West tells the story of the entire "Day of the Tourelles" in detail (*Saint Joan of Arc*, 168–74). At the retrial, Simon Charles testified that de Gaucourt had told him that his ugly scene with Joan had taken place on May 6, the day of the attack on the Augustins, not May 7, the day of the attack on the Tourelles. However, as Gies points out, this does not make sense. De Gaucourt had been present at the war council on May 5 in which Joan's tantrum resulted in her co-commanders agreeing to attack the next day, that is, May 6, when the French took the Augustins. It was during the night of

May 6–7, after they had taken the Augustins, that the male French captains decided to postpone any further attacks until more reinforcements arrived from the Dauphin. This was the decision that caused de Gaucourt to place himself at the city gate on the morning of May 7 to prevent any French troops from going out to make an unauthorized attack—until Joan showed up to overrule him in humiliating fashion, as has been described.

46. Duparc, *Procès en nullité de la condemnation*, 1:482; and Lucie-Smith, *Joan of Arc*, 117.

47. Quicherat, *Procès de condemnation et de réhabilitation*, 4:161–62, 5:293–94; Sackville-West, *Saint Joan of Arc*, 173–74; Gies, *Joan of Arc: The Legend*, 80–81; and Lucie-Smith, *Joan of Arc*, 119–20.

48. Duparc, *Procès en nullité de la condemnation*, 4:6, 50, 77; Sackville-West, *Saint Joan of Arc*, 173–74; Gies, *Joan of Arc: The Legend*, 80–81; and Lucie-Smith, *Joan of Arc*, 120.

49. Duparc, *Procès en nullité de la condemnation*, 4:6

50. Quicherat, *Procès de condemnation et de réhabilitation*, 4:163; Duparc, *Procès en nullité de la condemnation*, 4:6; Sackville-West, *Saint Joan of Arc*, 174; Gies, *Joan of Arc: The Legend*, 81; and Lucie-Smith, *Joan of Arc*, 121–22.

51. Duparc, *Procès en nullité de la condemnation*, 4:6–7, 17, 20–21, 91; Quicherat, *Procès de condemnation et de réhabilitation*, 4:163–65, 231–33; Sackville-West, *Saint Joan of Arc*, 177–78; Gies, *Joan of Arc: The Legend*, 81–82; and Lucie-Smith, *Joan of Arc*, 122–24.

52. Sackville-West, *Saint Joan of Arc*, 156.

53. Lucie-Smith, *Joan of Arc*, 123; also, Gies makes the same argument, *Joan of Arc: The Legend*, 81–82.

54. Pernoud and Clin, *Joan of Arc: Her Story*, 228–29. The previous February, the Bastard had been wounded in the fruitless assaults the French had made on a prepared English defensive position at the disastrous Battle of Rouvray, also known as "The Battle of the Herrings," named for the barrels of herrings that the English made into an improvised fort.

55. Philippe Contamine, "Les armées française et anglaise a l'époque de Jeanne d'Arc," *Revue des sociétés savantes de haute normandie* 57 (1970): 6; and Burne, *Agincourt War*, 225, 234.

56. After their losses at the Tourelles and elsewhere, the English had not quite 4,000 men. The French had about 6,000 men if we add together the Orléans city garrison of about 2,000 and Joan's rescue army of about 4,000. Burne, *Agincourt War*, 229, 237.

57. The anecdote about Joan promising her friends to return via the bridge is found in the retrial testimony in Duparc, *Procès en nullité de la condemnation*, 4:89, 91. See also Quicherat, *Procès de condemnation et de réhabilitation*, 4:227; Sackville-West, *Saint Joan of Arc*, 169; Gies, *Joan of Arc: The Legend*, 78; and Lucie-Smith, *Joan of Arc*, 116.

58. Duparc, *Procès en nullité de la condemnation*, 4:7–9.

59. Ibid.

60. Duparc, *Procès en nullité de la condemnation*, 3:277.

61. Edouard Perroy, *The Hundred Years War*, trans. W.B. Wells (New York: Capricorn Books, 1965), 243; and Sackville-West, *Saint Joan of Arc*, 24–26.

62. Duparc, *Procès en nullité de la condemnation*, 4:7–9; and Sackville-West, *Saint Joan of Arc*, 178–80.

63. Régine Pernoud, *Joan of Arc by Herself and Her Witnesses*, trans. Edward Hyams (N.p.: Stein and Day, 1966; reprint, New York: Scarborough House, 1994) (page citations are to the reprint edition), 110.

64. Quicherat, *Procès de condemnation et de réhabilitation*, 4:169.

65. The narrative of Joan's career from the assault on Jargeau through and including the Battle of Patay is found in Sackville-West, *Saint Joan of Arc*, 180–90; Gies, *Joan of Arc: The Legend*, 91–100; and Lucie-Smith, *Joan of Arc*, 129–47.

66. Quicherat, *Procès de condemnation et de réhabilitation*, 4:170; Duparc, *Procès en nullité de la condemnation*, 4:66–67; and Burne, *Agincourt War*, 250–51.

67. Kelly DeVries, *Joan of Arc: A Military Leader* (Gloustershire, England: Sutton Publishing, 1999), 104.

68. Burne, *Agincourt War*, 251–52.

69. Duparc, *Procès en nullité de la condemnation*, 4:67–68.

70. Burne, *Agincourt War*, 252.

71. Ibid., 252–54.

72. Ibid., 254–55; and Lucie-Smith, *Joan of Arc*, 137.

73. Burne, *Agincourt War*, 255.

74. Duparc, *Procès en nullité de la condemnation*, 4:50.

75. For discussion of the Battle of Patay, including numbers of troops involved and numbers of casualties, see DeVries, *Joan of Arc: A Military Leader*, 116–21; Burne, *Agincourt War*, 253, 256–61; Sackville-West, *Saint Joan of Arc*, 186–90; Gies, *Joan of Arc: The Legend*, 98–100; and Lucie-Smith, *Joan of Arc*, 141–47.

76. Duparc, *Procès en nullité de la condemnation*, 4:69.

77. Quicherat, *Procès de condemnation et de réhabilitation*, 4:375–76; Burne, *Agincourt War*, 260; and Sackville-West, *Saint Joan of Arc*, 189.

78. Duparc, *Procès en nullité de la condemnation*, 4:70.

79. Lieutenant-Colonel de Lancesseur, *Jeanne d'Arc, Chef de Guerre: Le génie militaire et politique de Jeanne d'Arc, Campagne de France 1429–1430* (Paris: Nouvelles Éditions Debresse, 1961), 75–76; and Michel de Lombarès, "Patay 18 Juin 1429," *Revue historique de l'armée* 22 (1966): 14–16. The account of Patay in de Liocourt agrees in its essential points with de Lombarès (Colonel Ferdinand de Liocourt, *La mission de Jeanne d'Arc*, 2 vols. [Paris: Nouvelles Éditions Latines, 1974], 2:143–47).

80. Quicherat, *Procès de condemnation et de réhabilitation*, 4:13; Sackville-West, *Saint Joan of Arc*, 183–84; and Gies, *Joan of Arc: The Legend*, 94.

81. De Liocourt, *La mission de Jeanne d'Arc*, 2:133.
82. Pernoud and Clin, *Joan of Arc: Her Story*, 190, 198–200.
83. Lucie-Smith, *Joan of Arc*, 49–50.
84. Duparc, *Procès en nullité de la condamnation*, 4:68.
85. Ibid., 4:68–69; and de Liocourt, *La mission de Jeanne d'Arc*, 2:150.
86. Duparc, *Procès en nullité de la condamnation*, 4:69.
87. Ibid., 4:7–8.
88. The narrative of Joan's career from the start of the march on Reims through and including Charles's coronation is found in Sackville-West, *Saint Joan of Arc*, 192–99; Gies, *Joan of Arc: The Legend*, 104–12; and Lucie-Smith, *Joan of Arc*, 148–64.
89. Quicherat, *Procès de condemnation et de réhabilitation*, 4:17–18; Sackville-West, *Saint Joan of Arc*, 190–92; Gies, *Joan of Arc: The Legend*, 106; and Lucie-Smith, *Joan of Arc*, 148.
90. Quicherat, *Procès de condemnation et de réhabilitation*, 4:180; Gies, *Joan of Arc: The Legend*, 105; and Lucie-Smith, *Joan of Arc*, 149.
91. Duparc, *Procès en nullité de la condamnation*, 4:9.
92. Quicherat, *Procès de condemnation et de réhabilitation*, 4:75–76.
93. Duparc, *Procès en nullité de la condamnation*, 4:83.
94. Quicherat, *Procès de condemnation et de réhabilitation*, 4:252; Gies, *Joan of Arc: The Legend*, 108–9; and Lucie-Smith, *Joan of Arc*, 155–56.
95. Pernoud, *Joan of Arc by Herself*, 120; and Quicherat, *Procès de condemnation et de réhabilitation*, 5:126–27.
96. The narrative of Joan's career—from Charles's coronation, through and including d'Alençon's failed effort to have Joan join him in Normandy—is found in Sackville-West, *Saint Joan of Arc*, 199–210; Gies, *Joan of Arc: The Legend*, 113–28; and Lucie-Smith, *Joan of Arc*, 165–84.
97. Quicherat, *Procès de condemnation et de réhabilitation*, 5:139–40; and Pernoud and Clin, *Joan of Arc: Her Story*, 254–55.
98. Quicherat, *Procès de condemnation et de réhabilitation*, 4:195; Sackville-West, *Saint Joan of Arc*, 203–4; Gies, *Joan of Arc: The Legend*, 120–21; and Lucie-Smith, *Joan of Arc*, 166–69.
99. Quicherat, *Procès de condemnation et de réhabilitation*, 4:26–27, 198–99, and 464–66; Pernoud, *Joan of Arc by Herself*, 60; Sackville-West, *Saint Joan of Arc*, 206–8; Gies, *Joan of Arc: The Legend*, 123–26; and Lucie-Smith, *Joan of Arc*, 177–79.
100. Quicherat, *Procès de condemnation et de réhabilitation*, 4:27–30; Pernoud, *Joan of Arc by Herself*, 141–42; Sackville-West, *Saint Joan of Arc*, 208–10; Gies, *Joan of Arc: The Legend*, 126–28; and Lucie-Smith, *Joan of Arc*, 179–81, 184. Burne, writing of Charles's betrayal of Joan at Paris, states that "The Maid of Orléans had been deliberately left in the lurch." Burne opines that this betrayal resulted from the machination of the anti-Joan diplomatic clique that formed Charles's inner circle of advisors. He states that "La Trémoïlle was probably 'the villain in the piece.'" (*Agincourt War*, 263). Sackville-West declares that

Charles's "destruction of d'Alençon's bridge was an act of overt treachery" (*Saint Joan of Arc,* 208).

101. Pernoud and Clin, *Joan of Arc: Her Story,* 84–85; and Lucie-Smith, *Joan of Arc,* 189, 196.

102. Duparc, *Procès en nullité de la condemnation,* 1:484–85; 4:15; Sackville-West, *Saint Joan of Arc,* 213–14; Gies, *Joan of Arc: The Legend,* 131–32; and Lucie-Smith, *Joan of Arc,* 187–89.

103. Quicherat, *Procès de condemnation et de réhabilitation,* 5:147–48; and Pernoud and Clin, *Joan of Arc: Her Story,* 81, 256–57.

104. Sackville-West, *Saint Joan of Arc,* 214–15, 219–20; Gies, *Joan of Arc: The Legend,* 132–34; Lucie-Smith, *Joan of Arc,* 189–91, 193; and Pernoud and Clin, *Joan of Arc: Her Story,* 81–82.

105. Pierre Tisset and Yvonne Lanhers, eds. and trans., *Procès de condemnation de Jeanne d'Arc,* 3 vols. (Paris: Klincksieck, 1960–71), 2:130–31; Sackville-West, *Saint Joan of Arc,* 224; Gies, *Joan of Arc: The Legend,* 137–38; and Lucie-Smith, *Joan of Arc,* 197–98.

106. The never-enthralled Edouard Perroy states that "it is permissible to doubt" that Joan turned the tide of the war. However, Perroy tries to have it both ways when he subsequently states that by handing the English their first major defeats and by orchestrating the coronation of Charles, "Joan of Arc's intervention was decisive, and the page she wrote, contrary to all expectation, in the history of France deserves to be remembered as one of the finest." Perroy, *The Hundred Years War,* 279, 281. Alfred H. Burne's *Agincourt War* is a blatantly Anglocentric work, but even Burne pays Joan this homage in the reprint edition: "But all the credit for starting the pendulum in its backward swing, and for starting it in no uncertain manner, must go to that marvelous soul, the pure and peerless Maid of Orléans" (267).

107. The following summary of the Hundred Years' War after Joan left the scene is derived from Burne, *Agincourt War,* 272–345.

108. This summary of the reform of the French army is derived from R. Earnest Dupuy and Trevor N. Dupuy, *The Harper Encyclopedia of Military History,* 4th ed. (New York: Harper Collins, 1993), 443–44, 452–53, 460–61. See also Philippe Contamine, *War in the Middle Ages,* trans. Michael Jones (New York: Barnes and Noble, 1998), 168–70; Major-General J.F.C. Fuller, *A Military History of the Western World: From the Earliest Times to the Battle of Lepanto* (New York: Funk and Wagnalls, 1954), 494–95; and Pernoud and Clin, *Joan of Arc: Her Story,* 167, 199.

109. Burne, *Agincourt War,* 307–45; and Pernoud and Clin, *Joan of Arc: Her Story,* 180–81, 198–200.

110. Duparc, *Procès en nullité de la condemnation,* 4:4, 74.

111. Duparc, *Procès en nullité de la condemnation,* 1:482–84; and 4:6, 49–50, 77.

112. Pernoud and Clin, *Joan of Arc: Her Story,* 173; and Régine Pernoud, *The Retrial of Joan of Arc: The Evidence at the Trial for Her Rehabilitation,*

1450–1456, trans. J.M. Cohen, with a foreword by Katherine Anne Porter (New York: Harcourt, Brace and Co., 1955), 135.

CHAPTER 7: JOAN'S LEADERSHIP QUALITIES: THE FIRST PART OF "HOW"

1. V. Sackville-West, *Saint Joan of Arc,* rev. ed. (London: Michael Joseph, 1948), 32–33; Frances Gies, *Joan of Arc: The Legend and the Reality* (New York: Harper & Row, 1981), 30; Edward A. Lucie-Smith, *Joan of Arc* (New York: W.W. Norton, 1977), 6–7; and Régine Pernoud and Marie-Véronique Clin, *Joan of Arc: Her Story,* trans. and rev. Jeremy du Quesnay Adams (New York: St. Martin's Press, 1998), 221.

2. Gies, *Joan of Arc: The Legend,* 20; and Lucie-Smith, *Joan of Arc,* 6, 9.

3. Sackville-West, *Saint Joan of Arc,* 34, 325.

4. Ibid., 33–35.

5. Nicholas Wright, *Knights and Peasants: The Hundred Years War in the French Countryside* (Woodbridge, England: Boydell Press, 1998), 114–15.

6. Gies presents a minutely detailed narrative of Joan's trial for heresy (*Joan of Arc: The Legend,* 152–224); Pernoud and Clin offer capsule biographies of twenty-five of her judges (*Joan of Arc: Her Story,* 206–17). After Bishop Cauchon ordered the trial moved from public to closed chambers, the number of clerics actually present at each session was far fewer than the original sixty or so.

7. Régine Pernoud, *The Retrial of Joan of Arc: The Evidence at the Trial for Her Rehabilitation, 1450–1456,* trans. J.M. Cohen, with a foreword by Katherine Anne Porter (New York: Harcourt, Brace and Co., 1955), 45–50.

8. Pierre Tisset and Yvonne Lanhers, eds. and trans., *Procès de condemnation de Jeanne d'Arc,* 3 vols. (Paris: Klincksieck, 1960–71), 2:140; and W.S. Scott, *Jeanne d'Arc* (London: Harrap, 1974), 134.

9. Tisset and Lanhers, *Procès de condemnation de Jeanne d'Arc,* 2:63; Pierre Duparc, ed., *Procès en nullité de la condemnation de Jeanne d'Arc,* 5 vols. (Paris: Klincksieck, 1977–89), 4:118; Scott, *Jeanne d'Arc,* 134–35; Lucie-Smith, *Joan of Arc,* 239; and Gies, *Joan of Arc: The Legend,* 166.

10. Duparc, *Procès en nullité de la condemnation,* 4:148; and Gies, *Joan of Arc: The Legend,* 160. For an analysis of Joan's tour de force performance at her trial, see Karen Sullivan, *The Interrogation of Joan of Arc* (Minneapolis: University of Minnesota Press, 1999), 99–105.

11. Duparc, *Procès en nullité de la condemnation,* 4:70; and Jules Quicherat, ed., *Procès de condemnation et de réhabilitation de Jeanne d'Arc dite la Pucelle,* 5 vols. (Paris: Chez Jules Renouard et Cie, 1841–49; reprint, New York: Johnson Reprint Corp., 1965), 4:75–76.

12. Joseph Jobé, ed., *Guns: An Illustrated History of Artillery* (New York: Crescent Books, 1971), 41. This book never mentions Joan, but it does offer a

primer on some of the basic artillery techniques of the late Middle Ages with which Joan very probably became acquainted.

13. This discussion of social-class considerations working to Joan's benefit in her relationship with her gunners is pure speculation on my part. I had already been thinking and writing with regard to this piece of speculation for some time when I discovered that I was speculating in good company. In his recent book, *Joan of Arc: A Military Leader* (Gloustershire, England: Sutton Publishing, 1999), Kelly DeVries offers the same educated guess, 56. This educated guess is one of the few brief pieces of speculation DeVries offers with regard to the "how" of Joan's military career.

14. Lieutenant-Colonel Alfred H. Burne, *The Agincourt War: A Military History of the Latter Part of the Hundred Years War from 1369 to 1453* (N.p.: Eyre and Spottiswoode, 1956; reprint, Ware, England: Wordsworth, 1999), 266.

15. John I. Alger, *Definitions and Doctrine of the Military Art,* West Point Military History Series, ed. Thomas E. Griess (Wayne, N.J.: Avery, 1985), 8–9; and United States Army, *Field Manual 100–5: Operations* (Washington, D.C.: Headquarters, Department of the Army, 1986), 173.

16. The following description of each principle of war is derived from United States Army, *Field Manual 100–5: Operations,* 97, 173–77 (more recent editions substitute "tempo" for "speed").

17. For example, General Schwarzkopf's self-defined objective in the Persian Gulf War of 1991 was the annihilation of the elite Iraqi Republican Guard. He knew that the Republican Guard was the only unit of Iraqi troops capable of causing serious harm to his own troops and also that the Guard formed Saddam Hussein's power base without which he would fall. Sometimes the objective can be more subtle. The objective of the North Vietnamese and the Viet Cong was to erode the will of the American voting public to continue the Vietnam War.

18. Alger, *Definitions and Doctrine of the Military Art,* 9.

19. Elmer C. May, Gerald P. Stadler, and John F. Votaw, *Ancient and Medieval Warfare,* West Point Military History Series, ed. Thomas E. Griess (Wayne, N.J.: Avery, 1984), 37, 59.

20. Albert Sidney Britt III, Jerome A. O'Connell, Dave Richard Palmer, and Gerald P. Stadler, *The Dawn of Modern Warfare,* West Point Military History Series, ed. Thomas E. Griess (Wayne, N.J.: Avery, 1984), 81, 84, 124.

21. Christine de Pizan, *The Book of Deeds of Arms and of Chivalry,* trans. Sumner Willard; ed. and with an introduction by Charity Cannon Willard (University Park, Pa.: Pennsylvania State University Press, 1999).

22. De Pizan, *Book of Deeds,* 79.

23. Ibid., 79.

24. Ibid., 71–74.

25. Ibid., 38–39, 41–43.

26. Ibid., 61–63.

27. Duparc, *Procès en nullité de la condemnation,* 4:69, 81, 151.

28. R. Earnest Dupuy and Trevor N. Dupuy, *The Harper Encyclopedia of Military History,* 4th ed. (New York: Harper Collins, 1993), 196–97; Pernoud and Clin, *Joan of Arc: Her Story,* 65, 144, 169; Sackville-West, *Saint Joan of Arc,* 191–92; and Gies, *Joan of Arc: The Legend,* 103.

29. Duparc, *Procès en nullité de la condemnation,* 4:69; and Régine Pernoud, *Joan of Arc by Herself and Her Witnesses,* trans. Edward Hyams (N.p.: Stein and Day, 1966; reprint, New York: Scarborough House, 1994) (page citations are to the reprint edition), 141.

30. These examples of Joan's mania for speed come from the retrial testimony of d'Aulon, the Bastard, and d'Alençon. See Duparc, *Procès en nullité de la condemnation,* 1:482; and 4:7–9, 66–67, 69. Also see DeVries, *Joan of Arc: A Military Leader,* 97–101, 116, for more cogent discussion of speed as a factor in Joan's military operations. As DeVries points out, the *Journal of the Siege of Orléans,* the *Chronicle of the Maid,* and the chronicle written by Jean Chartier all stress the great haste with which the French army moved out to pursue the English toward Patay. These three works were written during or shortly after Joan's lifetime. See Quicherat, *Procès de condemnation et de réhabilitation,* 4:67–68, 176, 242.

31. Duparc, *Procès en nullité de la condemnation,* 4:150–51.

32. Ibid., 4:67.

33. Ibid., 4:66; and Lucie-Smith, *Joan of Arc,* 130.

34. Gies, *Joan of Arc: The Legend,* 85.

35. Gervase Phillips, Admissions Tutor, Historical Studies, Department of History and Economic History, Manchester Metropolitan University, electronic mail message to the author, August 5, 1999.

36. Marina Warner, *Joan of Arc: The Image of Female Heroism* (London: Weidenfeld and Nicolson), 1981.

37. Ibid., 139–58.

38. Sackville-West, *Saint Joan of Arc,* 19–20.

39. Warner, *Joan of Arc: The Image of Female Heroism,* 145–46.

40. Ibid., 157.

41. Ibid., 161.

42. Ibid., 160–70.

43. This discussion of Joan's sword is summarized from Tisset and Lanhers, *Procès de condemnation de Jeanne d'Arc,* 2:75–76; Warner, *Joan of Arc: The Image of Female Heroism,* 164–65; Pernoud and Clin, *Joan of Arc: Her Story,* 225–26; Sackville-West, *Saint Joan of Arc,* 131–32; Gies, *Joan of Arc: The Legend,* 60; and Lucie-Smith, *Joan of Arc,* 84–85.

44. Duparc, *Procès en nullité de la condemnation,* 4:51, 69–70; Quicherat, *Procès de condemnation et de réhabilitation,* 4:71–72, 93; Pernoud and Clin, *Joan of Arc: Her Story,* 225–26; Sackville-West, *Saint Joan of Arc,* 224–25; and Lucie-Smith, *Joan of Arc,* 176.

45. Tisset and Lanhers, *Procès de condemnation de Jeanne d'Arc,* 2:77–78, 142–43; Duparc, *Procès en nullité de la condemnation,* 4:72–73; Warner, *Joan of Arc: The Image of Female Heroism,* 165–68; Colonel Ferdinand de Liocourt, *La mission de Jeanne d'Arc,* 2 vols. (Paris: Nouvelles Éditions Latines, 1974), 1:284–85; Sackville-West, *Saint Joan of Arc,* 132; Gies, *Joan of Arc: The Legend,* 59; and Lucie-Smith, *Joan of Arc,* 85–87.

46. Duparc, *Procès en nullité de la condemnation,* 4:61.

47. Warner, *Joan of Arc: The Image of Female Heroism,* 77–95.

48. Jane Marie Pinzino, "Heretic or Holy Woman? Cultural Representation and Gender in the Trial to Rehabilitate Joan of Arc" (Ph.D. diss., University of Pennsylvania, 1996).

49. Ibid., 40.

50. Ibid., 147–49, 153–57.

51. Ibid., 147–53.

52. From this point on, my argument is admittedly speculative—but not totally. I served for twenty years as a soldier in the gender-integrated United States Army of the 1970s, 1980s, and 1990s. I fully acknowledge the risks inherent in trying to read anecdotal evidence from the present into the past. But I was a keen observer of how many men and a few women interact in a military subculture and I think this gives me at least a glimmer of the chemistry that existed between Joan and her cohorts.

53. Duparc, *Procès en nullité de la condemnation,* 4:47, 64.

54. Quicherat, *Procès de condemnation et de réhabilitation,* 5:107.

55. Duparc, *Procès en nullité de la condemnation,* 4:62.

56. Ibid., 4:70.

57. Ibid., 4:85.

58. Sackville-West, *Saint Joan of Arc,* 154, 170–71.

59. This passage by de Boulainvilliers is found in Latin in Quicherat, *Procès de condemnation et de réhabilitation,* 5:120. It can be found translated into English in Pernoud, *Joan of Arc by Herself,* 98–99.

60. Duparc, *Procès en nullité de la condemnation,* 4:50, 75, 77–78; and Sackville-West, *Saint Joan of Arc,* 20, 189–90. At her trial, Joan proclaimed that she carried her banner into battle in order to avoid killing anyone with her sword and that she had never killed anyone (Tisset and Lanhers, *Procès de condemnation de Jeanne d'Arc,* 2:77–78). This statement by Joan seems a bit disingenuous when one considers that she knowingly gave the orders that resulted in thousands of men being killed. This little piece of seeming hypocrisy on Joan's part may be the only stain that a historian can make stick to her apparently flawless moral character. However, it should be borne in mind that being a commander has not always entailed—and does not presently entail—hacking about in the thick of the fight like a private soldier.

61. Gies, *Joan of Arc: The Legend,* 93; also see Pernoud, *The Retrial of Joan of Arc,* 134–35; Duparc, *Procès en nullité de la condemnation,* 4:67; and Quicherat, *Procès de condemnation et de réhabilitation,* 4:10–11, 13.

62. Duparc, *Procès en nullité de la condemnation,* 4:52. In the original transcripts of the retrial, the testimony of the witnesses is rendered in the third person, i.e., "the witness said this and the witness said that." I have taken the liberty of translating the testimony in the first person.

63. Quicherat, *Procès de condemnation et de réhabilitation,* 5:107.

64. These comments by Joan's intimates concerning her sexuality and their responses to it are all from Duparc, *Procès en nullité de la condemnation.* The pages containing the relevant testimony of each of these men are as follows: d'Aulon, 1:486; de Metz, 3:278; de Poulengy, 3:293; Thibault, 4:54; and d'Alençon, 4:70.

65. Kelly DeVries comes to the same conclusion about the eternal nature of soldierly lechery in *Joan of Arc: A Military Leader,* 33.

66. Lucie-Smith, *Joan of Arc,* 183.

67. Duparc, *Procès en nullité de la condemnation,* 4:59.

68. Quicherat, *Procès de condemnation et de réhabilitation,* 5:293.

CHAPTER 8: JOAN'S LUCKY CIRCUMSTANCES: THE SECOND PART OF "HOW"

1. Deborah A. Fraioli, *Joan of Arc: The Early Debate* (Woodbridge, England: Boydell Press, 2000), 55–68; Jane Marie Pinzino, "Heretic or Holy Woman? Cultural Representation and Gender in the Trial to Rehabilitate Joan of Arc" (Ph.D. diss., University of Pennsylvania, 1996), 145–46; Colonel Ferdinand de Liocourt, *La mission de Jeanne d'Arc,* 2 vols. (Paris: Nouvelles Éditions Latines, 1974), 1:179–80; and Pierre Duparc, ed., *Procès en nullité de la condemnation de Jeanne d'Arc,* 5 vols. (Paris: Klincksieck, 1977–89), 3:283, 285.

2. Régine Pernoud and Marie-Véronique Clin, *Joan of Arc: Her Story,* trans. and rev. Jeremy du Quesnay Adams (New York: St. Martin's Press, 1998), 197; and Jules Quicherat, ed., *Procès de condemnation et de réhabilitation de Jeanne d'Arc dite la Pucelle,* 5 vols. (Paris: Chez Jules Renouard et Cie, 1841–49; reprint, New York: Johnson Reprint Corp., 1965), 5:3–21.

3. Tim Newark, *Women Warlords* (London: Blandford Press, 1989), 98–104, 113–21. This book is admittedly a work of "pop" history, but it is still useful for obtaining the basic facts about women such as Matilda of Tuscany and Jeanne de Montfort. Newark's bibliography cites the *Vita Mathildis celebirrimae principis Italiae* by Donizo as the twelfth-century primary source about Matilda of Tuscany. The same bibliography cites Froissart's *Chronicles of England, France, and Spain* as the period primary source about Jeanne de Montfort. Also, see Frances Gies, *Joan of Arc: The Legend and the Reality* (New York: Harper & Row, 1981), 88.

4. Pernoud and Clin, *Joan of Arc: Her Story,* 183–84; and Quicherat, *Procès de condemnation et de réhabilitation,* 3:400–401. I am indebted to Reverend

Monsignor Perron J. Auve of Saint Andrew's Church in Ellensburg, Washington, for his help translating the Latin of Gélu's treatise into English.

5. Quicherat, *Procès de condemnation et de réhabilitation,* 5:11–12.

6. Charles Oman, *The Art of War in the Middle Ages,* A.D. *378–1515,* rev. and ed. John H. Beeler (Ithaca, N.Y.: Cornell University Press, 1953; reprint, Cornell Paperbacks, 1968), 57–72.

7. Da Legnano and Bonet, in their mammoth tomes about morality in the conduct of war, gave a scant few pages to the practical aspects of how-to-win military theory. Giovanni da Legnano, *Tractatus de Bello, de Represaliis et de Duello* [Tractate on War, Reprisals, and the Duel], trans. James Leslie Brierly and ed. Thomas Erskine Holland (Oxford: Oxford University Press, 1917), 235–37; and Honoré Bonet, *Arbre des Batailles* [The Tree of Battles], trans. G. W. Coopland (Cambridge, Mass.: Harvard University Press, 1949), 130–32.

8. Phillipe Contamine, *War in the Middle Ages,* trans. Michael Jones (New York: Barnes and Noble, 1998), 210–18; and R. Earnest Dupuy and Trevor N. Dupuy, *The Harper Encyclopedia of Military History,* 4th ed. (New York: Harper Collins, 1993), 434–35.

9. Pernoud and Clin, *Joan of Arc: Her Story,* present capsule biographies of these five comrades of Joan on 172–73, 180–81, 187–88, 198–200, and 206 respectively.

10. Pernoud and Clin, *Joan of Arc: Her Story,* 228–30; and Charles Oman, *A History of the Art of War in the Middle Ages,* vol. 2, *1278–1485,* 2nd ed. (London: Methuen and Co., 1924), 393–94. Burne has essentially the same assessment as Oman with regard to the flawed English deployment at Orléans. Burne goes on to say that after the fighting at Orléans, the English again failed to concentrate and "stupidly" dispersed their forces to Jargeau, Meung, and Beaugency. These isolated English garrisons then became easy pickings for Joan in her next campaign. Lieutenant-Colonel Alfred H. Burne, *The Agincourt War: A Military History of the Latter Part of the Hundred Years War from 1369 to 1453* (N.p.: Eyre and Spottiswoode, 1956; reprint, Ware, England: Wordsworth, 1999), 240, 246–48, 250. See also Philippe Contamine, "Les armées française et anglaise a l'époque de Jeanne d'Arc," *Revue des sociétés savantes de haute normandie* 57 (1970): 6–7, where he provides a brief sketch of the course of the siege of Orléans prior to Joan's arrival. In the same article, he also quotes a French veteran of the siege, Jean de Bueil, who harshly criticized the English for their use of the faulty technique of splitting their forces between forts spaced around the city (ibid., 19).

CHAPTER 9: SUMMATION

1. Katherine Anne Porter, foreword to Régine Pernoud, *The Retrial of Joan of Arc: The Evidence at the Trial for Her Rehabilitation, 1450–1456,* trans. J. M. Cohen (New York: Harcourt, Brace and Co.), viii.

APPENDIX A: JOAN'S FOUR KEY MISSIONS OR PROPHECIES

1. Pierre Duparc, ed., *Procès en nullité de la condemnation de Jeanne d'Arc*, 5 vols. (Paris: Klincksieck, 1977–89), 4:81
2. Ibid., 4:151.
3. Ibid., 4:69.

APPENDIX B: JOAN OF ARC AT THE MOVIES

1. Kevin J. Harty, "Jeanne au Cinéma," in *Fresh Verdicts on Joan of Arc,* ed. Bonnie Wheeler and Charles T. Wood (New York: Garland Publishing, 1996), 237.

APPENDIX C: JOAN'S PERSONAL APPEARANCE

1. Kelly DeVries, *Joan of Arc: A Military Leader* (Gloustershire, England: Sutton Publishing, 1999), 31–32.
2. Frances Gies, *Joan of Arc: The Legend and the Reality* (New York: Harper & Row, 1981), 47–48; and V. Sackville-West, *Saint Joan of Arc,* rev. ed. (London: Michael Joseph, 1948), 18.
3. Jules Quicherat, ed., *Procès de condemnation et de réhabilitation de Jeanne d'Arc dite la Pucelle,* 5 vols. (Paris: Chez Jules Renouard et Cie, 1841–49; reprint, New York: Johnson Reprint Corp., 1965), 5:147; and Sackville-West, *Saint Joan of Arc,* 13–14.
4. Pierre Duparc, ed., *Procès en nullité de la condemnation de Jeanne d'Arc,* 5 vols. (Paris: Klincksieck, 1977–89), 3:277.
5. Duparc, *Procès en nullité de la condemnation,* 1:486; and 4:70.
6. Marie-Véronique Clin, "Joan of Arc and Her Doctors," in *Fresh Verdicts on Joan of Arc,* ed. Bonnie Wheeler and Charles T. Wood (New York: Garland Publishing, 1996), 299.
7. Duparc, *Procès en nullité de la condemnation,* 3:278; and 4:54.
8. Duparc, *Procès en nullité de la condemnation,* 4:86; and Gies, *Joan of Arc: The Legend,* 47, 149.

SELECTED BIBLIOGRAPHY

Alger, John I. *Definitions and Doctrine of the Military Art.* West Point Military History Series, edited by Thomas E. Griess. Wayne, N.J.: Avery, 1985.

Allmand, Christopher, ed. *Society at War: The Experience of England and France during the Hundred Years War.* Edinburgh: Oliver and Boyd, 1973. Reprint. Woodbridge, England: Boydell Press, 1998.

Bonet, Honoré. *Arbre des Batailles* [The Tree of Battles]. Translated by G. W. Coopland. Cambridge, Mass.: Harvard University Press, 1949.

Britt, Albert Sidney, III, Jerome A. O'Connell, Dave Richard Palmer, and Gerald P. Stadler. *The Dawn of Modern Warfare.* West Point Military History Series, edited by Thomas E. Griess. Wayne, N.J.: Avery, 1984.

Burne, Lieutenant-Colonel Alfred H. *The Agincourt War: A Military History of the Latter Part of the Hundred Years War from 1369 to 1453.* N.p.: Eyre and Spottiswoode, 1956. Reprint. Ware, England: Wordsworth, 1999.

———. *The Crécy War: A Military History of the Hundred Years War from 1337 to the Peace of Bretigny, 1360.* N.p.: Eyre and Spottiswoode, 1955. Reprint. Ware, England: Wordsworth, 1999.

Cantor, Norman F. *The Civilization of the Middle Ages.* New York: HarperCollins, 1993. Reprint. HarperPerennial, 1994.

Clin, Marie-Véronique. "Joan of Arc and Her Doctors." In *Fresh Verdicts on Joan of Arc,* edited by Bonnie Wheeler and Charles T. Wood, 295–302. New York: Garland Publishing, 1996.

Contamine, Philippe. "Les armées française et anglaise a l'époque de Jeanne d'Arc." *Revue des sociétés savantes de haute normandie* 57 (1970): 5–33.

———. "La guerre de siège au temps de Jeanne d'Arc." *Dossiers de archéologie* 34 (May 1979): 11–20.

———. *War in the Middle Ages.* Translated by Michael Jones. New York: Barnes and Noble, 1998.

DeVries, Kelly. *Joan of Arc: A Military Leader.* Gloustershire, England: Sutton Publishing, 1999.

———. "The Use of Gunpowder Weaponry by and against Joan of Arc during the Hundred Years War." *War and Society* 14 (May 1996): 1–15.

———. "A Woman as Leader of Men: Joan of Arc's Military Career." In *Fresh Verdicts on Joan of Arc,* edited by Bonnie Wheeler and Charles T. Wood, 3–18. New York: Garland Publishing, 1996.

Duparc, Pierre, ed. *Procès en nullité de la condemnation de Jeanne d'Arc.* 5 vols. Paris: Klincksieck, 1977–89.

Dupuy, R. Earnest, and Trevor N. Dupuy. *The Harper Encyclopedia of Military History.* 4th ed. New York: HarperCollins, 1993.

Fraioli, Deborah A. *Joan of Arc: The Early Debate.* Woodbridge, England: Boydell Press, 2000.

France, Anatole. *Vie de Jeanne d'Arc.* 2 vols. Paris: Calmann-Lévy, 1908.

Fuller, J.F.C. *A Military History of the Western World: From the Earliest Times to the Battle of Lepanto.* New York: Funk and Wagnalls, 1954.

Gies, Frances. *Joan of Arc: The Legend and the Reality.* New York: Harper & Row, 1981.

Gurevich, Aron. *Medieval Popular Culture: Problems of Belief and Perception.* Translated by János M. Bak and Paul A. Hollingsworth. Cambridge: Cambridge University Press, 1988. Reprint. Cambridge: Cambridge University Press, 1997.

Harty, Kevin J. "Jeanne au Cinéma." In *Fresh Verdicts on Joan of Arc,* edited by Bonnie Wheeler and Charles T. Wood, 237–264. New York: Garland Publishing, 1996.

Huizinga, Johan. "The Political and Military Significance of Chivalric Ideas in the Late Middle Ages." In *Men and Ideas, History, the Middle Ages, the Renaissance: Essays by Johan Huizinga.* Translated by James S. Holmes and Hans van Marle. New York: Meridian Books, 1959.

Jobé, Joseph, ed. *Guns: An Illustrated History of Artillery.* New York: Crescent Books, 1971.

Kaeuper, Richard W., and Elspeth Kennedy. *The Book of Chivalry of Geoffroi de Charny: Text, Context, and Translation.* Philadelphia: University of Pennsylvania Press, 1996.

Keegan, John. *The Face of Battle.* New York: Viking, 1976.

Lancesseur, Lieutenant-Colonel de. *Jeanne d'Arc, Chef de Guerre: Le génie militaire et politique de Jeanne d'Arc, Campagne de France 1429–1430.* Paris: Nouvelles Éditions Debresse, 1961.

Lang, Andrew. *The Maid of France: Being the Story of the Life and Death of Jeanne d'Arc.* London: Longman's, 1908.

Legnano, Giovanni da. *Tractatus de Bello, de Represaliis et de Duello* [Tractate on War, Reprisals, and the Duel]. Translated by James Leslie Brierly. Edited by Thomas Erskine Holland. Oxford: Oxford University Press, 1917.

Liddell Hart, B. H. *Strategy.* 2nd ed. New York: Signet, 1974.

Liocourt, Colonel Ferdinand de. *La mission de Jeanne d'Arc.* 2 vols. Paris: Nouvelles Éditions Latines, 1974.

Lombarès, Michel de. "Patay 18 Juin 1429." *Revue historique de l'armée* 22 (1966): 5–16.

Lucie-Smith, Edward A. *Joan of Arc.* New York: W. W. Norton, 1977.

Margolis, Nadia. *Joan of Arc in History, Literature, and Film.* New York: Garland Publishing, 1990.

May, Elmer C., Gerald P. Stadler, and John F. Votaw. *Ancient and Medieval Warfare.* West Point Military History Series, edited by Thomas E. Griess. Wayne, N.J.: Avery, 1984.

Michelet, Jules. "Jeanne d'Arc." In *Oeuvres Complètes: Etude du ms. et examen des remaniements du texte de 1841 et 1844 à travers les rééditions par Robert Casanova,* edited by Paul Viallaneix, 6:60–122. Paris: Flammarion, 1978.

Newark, Tim. *Women Warlords.* London: Blandford, 1989.

Nicolle, David. *Orléans 1429 France Turns the Tide.* Oxford: Osprey Publishing, 2001.

Oman, Charles. *The Art of War in the Middle Ages, A.D. 378–1515.* Revised and edited by John H. Beeler. Ithaca, New York: Cornell University Press, 1953. Reprint. New York: Cornell Paperbacks, 1968.

———. *A History of the Art of War in the Middle Ages.* Vol. 2, *1278–1485.* 2d ed. London: Methuen and Co., 1924.

Pernoud, Régine. *Joan of Arc by Herself and Her Witnesses.* Translated by Edward Hyams. N.p.: Stein and Day, 1966. Reprint. New York: Scarborough House, 1994.

———. *The Retrial of Joan of Arc: The Evidence at the Trial for Her Rehabilitation, 1450–1456.* Translated by J. M. Cohen. Foreword by Katherine Anne Porter. New York: Harcourt, Brace and Co., 1955.

———, and Marie-Véronique Clin. *Joan of Arc: Her Story.* Translated and revised by Jeremy du Quesnay Adams. New York: St. Martin's Press, 1998.

Perroy, Edouard. *The Hundred Years War.* Translated by W. B. Wells. New York: Capricorn Books, 1965.

Phillips, Gervase. E-mail message to the author, August 5, 1999.

Pinzino, Jane Marie. "Heretic or Holy Woman? Cultural Representation and Gender in the Trial to Rehabilitate Joan of Arc." Ph.D. diss., University of Pennsylvania, 1996.

———. "Just War, Joan of Arc and the Politics of Salvation." Unpublished manuscript. Tacoma, Wash.: University of Puget Sound, 2001.

Pizan, Christine de. *The Book of Deeds of Arms and of Chivalry.* Translated by Sumner Willard. Edited and with an introduction by Charity Cannon Willard. University Park, Pa.: Pennsylvania State University Press, 1999.

Quicherat, Jules, ed. *Procès de condemnation et de réhabilitation de Jeanne d'Arc dite la Pucelle.* 5 vols. Paris: Chez Jules Renouard et Cie, 1841–49. Reprint. New York: Johnson Reprint Corp., 1965.

Rothero, Christopher. *The Armies of Agincourt.* London: Osprey, 1981.

Sackville-West, V. *Saint Joan of Arc.* Rev. ed. London: Michael Joseph, 1948.

Scott, W. S. *Jeanne d'Arc.* London: Harrap, 1974.

Shaw, George Bernard. *Saint Joan.* New York: Brentano's, 1924.

Stephenson, Carl. *Medieval Feudalism.* Ithaca, N.Y.: Cornell University Press, 1942. Reprint. Ithaca, N.Y.: Cornell Paperbacks, 1965.

Sullivan, Karen. *The Interrogation of Joan of Arc.* Minneapolis: University of Minnesota Press, 1999.

Tisset, Pierre, and Yvonne Lanhers, eds. and trans. *Procès de condemnation de Jeanne d'Arc.* 3 vols. Paris: Klincksieck, 1960–71.

Trask, Willard, ed. and trans. *Joan of Arc in Her Own Words.* New York: Turtle Point Press, 1996. Note: This book was originally published with the title *Joan of Arc, A Self-Portrait.* New York: Stackpole, 1936.

Twain, Mark. *Personal Recollections of Joan of Arc.* New York: Harper's, 1896.

United States Army. *Field Manual 100–5: Operations.* Washington, D.C.: Headquarters, Department of the Army, 1986.

Warner, Marina. *Joan of Arc: The Image of Female Heroism.* London: Weidenfeld and Nicolson, 1981.

Wheeler, Bonnie, and Charles T. Wood, eds. *Fresh Verdicts on Joan of Arc.* New York: Garland Publishing, 1996.

Wright, Nicholas. *Knights and Peasants: The Hundred Years War in the French Countryside.* Woodbridge, England: Boydell Press, 1998.

INDEX

Administration, principle of, 94–95, 101
Agincourt, Battle of (1415), 17–22, 96
Alençon, Jean, duke of, 73, 119; assault on Jargeau and, 102; assault on Paris and, 80; Battle of Montépilloy and, 79; Battle of Patay and, 75; on courage and charisma of Joan of Arc, 109–10, 112; first meeting with Joan of Arc and, 32–34; Loire River campaign and, 67–71; retrial testimony of, 86–87, 105–6; as witness, 81
Alexander the Great, 95
Archetypes, Joan of Arc and, 103–9
Armagnac, Thibault d', 45–46
Arras, Franquet d', 83
Arras, Treaty of (1435), 84
Auberoche, Battle of (1345), 16
Augustine of Hippo, Saint, 40
Augustins, 49, 59, 65
Aulon, Jean d', 37, 42, 56–57, 112; testimony of, at retrial, 86

Banners, as symbols, Joan of Arc's use of, 106, 108
Barbin, Jean, 112

Bastard of Orléans (Jean, count of Dunois), 37, 42, 64, 119; Battle of Patay and, 75; as leader of new French army, 85; retrial testimony of, 63, 86–87; role of, in siege of Orléans, 50–52; as witness, 81
Baudricourt, Robert de, 28, 29
Baugé, Battle of (1421), 23
Beaugency, assault on, 69–70, 73, 100
Bedford, duke of, 23, 35, 71; effect of Joan of Arc on army of, 38–39
Bonet, Honoré, 40
Boucher, Jacques, 52
Boulainvilliers, Perceval de, 110–11
Bureau, Jean and Gaspard, 85
Burgundy, dukes of, 23
Burgundy, Philip, duke of: becomes ally of Charles VII, 84; Joan of Arc's letter to, 78. *See also* Burgundy, dukes of

Cagny, Perceval de, 8, 42, 43, 73, 111
Castillon, Battle of (1453), 85
Catholic Church, 4
Cauchon, Bishop Pierre, 90

Charles, Simon, 45, 60, 76–77
Charles VI, king of France, 23
Charles VII (Dauphin Charles), king of France, 1–2, 23, 66; coronation journey of, 75–78; creation of new French Army by, 84–85; crowning of, 66–67; importance of crowning, 98–99; journey to meet, at Chinon, 30–31; lack of money to pay soldiers and, 15; meeting with, at Chinon, 31–32; procrastination of, 99
Charny, Geoffroi de, 16, 40
Chartier, Jean, 8, 57, 76, 105–6
Chastellain, Georges, 41
Chinon, Joan of Arc's journey to castle of, 30–32
Clovis, 98
Compiègne, 41; Joan of Arc taken prisoner at, 4, 83
Contamine, Philippe, 118
Coutes, Louis de, 37, 42, 56; retrial testimony of, 86
Cravant, Battle of (1423), 23
Crécy, Battle of (1346), 16

Dauphin Charles. *See* Charles VII (Dauphin Charles), king of France
DeVries, Kelly, 11–12
Dunois, Jean, count of. *See* Bastard of Orléans (Jean, count of Dunois)
Duparc, Pierre, 8

Economy of force, principle of, 94
England: development of professional armies in, 15–16; effectiveness of armies of, 15; loss of Philip, duke of Burgundy's support and, 84; siege of Orléans and army of, 47–49

Fastolf, Sir John, 56, 65, 69–70
Feudal system, warfare and, 14. *See also* France, Medieval

Formigny, Battle of (1450), 85
Fraioli, Deborah A., 11
France, Anatole, 9
France: effectiveness of Medieval armies of, 16–17; in 1429, map; Medieval attitudes about war in, 15–16; power of prophecies in Medieval, 115–16
Frederick the Great, 95
Fuller, J. F. C., 93

Gamaches, Guillaume de, 110
Gaucourt, Raoul de, 60–61, 65, 80
Gélu, Jacques, 117
Gies, Frances, 5, 10, 111
Glasdale, Sir William, 61
Guesclin, Bertrand du, 17
Gunpowder artillery: French army and, 85; Joan of Arc's mastery of, 91–92

Hannibal, 95
Henry V, king of England, 17–23, 96, 97
Henry VI, king of England, 23, 98–99
Hire, La (Étienne de Vignolles), 41, 55, 59, 63, 97, 119; Battle of Patay and, 70–71, 72–73
Hundred Years' War, 13–14; battles during opening years of, 16–17; changes in warfare during, 14–15; feudal system during, 14

Isabeau of Bavaria, 66

Jargeau, assault on, 41, 67–69, 73, 100, 102
Jean, count of Dunois. *See* Bastard of Orléans (Jean, count of Dunois)
Jean, duke of Alençon. *See* Alençon, Jean, duke of
Joan of Arc, career of: canonization of, 4; Charles VII confers titles of

nobility on, 81–82; heresy trial of, 90–91; impact of end of serfdom on, 14; impact of Hundred Years' War on, 13–14; impact of organization of armies on, 14–15; journey to Dauphin's castle at Chinon, 30–31; meeting with Dauphin at Chinon and, 31–32; overview of life of, 1–4; summation of, 121; testing of, by Dauphin Charles, 34

Joan of Arc, character of: ability to make soldiers fight and, 41–42; effect of, on British army, 38–39; effect of, on French army, 37–38; gift of prophecy and, 36; impact of, on French social classes, 42–43; intellect of, 89–90; moral standards and, 39; willpower of, 89–90

Joan of Arc, childhood of, 25–26; first journey to Vaucouleurs to offer services, 26–28; second journey to Vaucouleurs to offer services, 28–30

Joan of Arc, as a leader: acceptance by men and, 116–17; courage and charisma of, 109–13; Ideal Androgyne archetype and, 103–4; Knight archetype and, 104–6; luck and, 116–20; Prophet archetype and, 107–9; sexuality of, 112–13; use of swords by, 105; use of words and symbols by, 102–9

Joan of Arc, as military commander, 45–46; approach to Orléans and, 49–51; assault on La Charité by, 81; assault on Paris and, 80; assault on Saint-Pierre-le-Moûtier by, 81; assessment of, 83–87; Battle of Lagny and, 83; Battle of Montépilloy and, 79; co-commanders and, 119; contribution of, to lifting of siege of Orléans, 64–65; coronation journey and, 75–78; doctrine of just war and, 40–41; Duke of Alençon and, 32–34; entrance into Orléans and, 52–53; goes to Blois to take charge of army, 36; goes to Tours, 36; influence on strategy and tactics by, 71–75; Loire River campaign and, 67–71; mastery of gunpowder artillery and, 91–92; military theory and, 97–98; principles of war and, 92–96, 97–99; siege of Orléans and, 49–66

Joan of Arc, scholarship on: historians' views of, 4–5; impact of, 4; literature review of, 7–12; military career of, 11–12; modern scholarship of, 8; retrial of, 7–8; secondary sources about, 8–9

Just war, doctrines of, 40

Knight archetype, Joan of Arc and, 104–6

La Hire. *See* Hire, La (Étienne de Vignolles)
La Trémoïlle, Georges de, 74, 79, 80
Lagny, Battle of, 83
Lancesseur, Lieutenant-Colonel de, 5, 11, 72
Lang, Andrew, 9, 10
Lanhers, Yvonne, 8
Laval, Guy de, 43, 109, 111
Laxart, Durand, 28
Legnano, Giovanni da, 40
Liocourt, Ferdinand de, 5, 11
Loire River campaign, 67–71
Lombarès, Michel de, 72–73
Longbow, 15
Lucie-Smith, Edward A., 10, 63
Luck, Joan of Arc and, 116–20

Maintenance of morale, principle of, 94, 99
Maneuver, principle of, 93–94, 101

INDEX

Margolis, Nadia, 9
Marlborough, duke of, 95
Martel, Charles, 105
Mass, principle of, 94, 101
Matilda of Tuscany, 116
Mauron, Battle of (1352), 16
Medieval France. *See* France
Mercenaries, 14–15
Metz, Jean de (Jean de Nouillompont), 29, 30, 37, 112
Meung, assault on, 69–70, 73–74, 100
Michelet, Jules, 9
Milet, Colette, 57
Military theory: de Pizan and, 95–96; Joan of Arc's knowledge of, 97; Middle Ages and, 118–19. *See also* Warfare
Montfort, Jeanne de, 116
Morlaix, Battle of (1342), 16

Napoleon Bonaparte, 73
Nouillompont, Jean de (Jean de Metz), 29, 30, 37, 112

Objective, principle of, 93
Offensive, principle of, 93, 99
Orléans, siege of, 23, 46–66; assault on Augustins, 59; assault on Saint Loup, 56–57, 64–65; capture of Tourelles, 59–63, 64; Joan of Arc's entrance into city, 52–54; role of the Bastard and, 50–52; ultimatums to English, 54–55

Paris, assault on, 80
Pasquerel, Brother Jean, 37; battle for Saint Loup and, 57; retrial testimony of, 60, 86
Patay, assault on, 70–71, 74–75, 97, 100–101
Pernoud, Régine, 10
Perroy, Edouard, 5
Pinzino, Jane Marie, 40, 108

Pizan, Christine de, 96, 116, 117, 119
Poitiers, Battle of (1356), 16
Pontoise, assault on, 84
Porter, Katherine Ann, 121
Poulengy, Bertrand de, 30, 37, 112
Prophet archetype, Joan of Arc and, 106–9

Quicherat, Jules, 8

Richemont, Arthur de, 74, 80, 119; as leader of new French army, 85
Roman Catholic Church. *See* Catholic Church
Rouvray, Battle of (1429), 29–30

Sackville-West, Victoria, 9–10
Saint-Catherine-de-Fierbois, sword of, 105–6
Saint Jean Le Blanc fort, 65
Saint Loup, assault on, 57, 64–65
Saint-Pierre-le-Moûtier, assault on, 81
Security, principle of, 94
Seguin, Seguin de, 102
Shaw, George Bernard, 39
Simplicity, principle of, 94
Sluys, Battle of (1340), 16
Speed, principle of, 93, 99
Strategy, Joan of Arc's knowledge of, 71–73, 100
Sullivan, Karen, 10–11
Surprise, principle, 94
Swords, as symbols, Joan of Arc's use of, 105

Tactics, Joan of Arc's use of, 71–73, 100
Talbot, Lord John, 50, 69–70; Battle of Patay and, 71
Thibault, Gobert, 111
Tisset, Pierre, 8
Tourelles, 65; assault on, 59–62; loss of, to English, 47

Touroulde, Marguerite La, 107, 109
Troyes, assault on, 75–78
Troyes, Treaty of (1420), 23, 66
Twain, Mark, 9

Unity of command, principle of, 94, 101

Vegetius, 96, 118
Verneuil, Battle of (1424), 23
Vignolles, Étienne de (La Hire). *See* Hire, La (Étienne de Vignolles)

Warfare: changes in, during Hundred Years' War, 14–15; doctrines of just war and, 40–41; principles of, 92–96; simplicity of, in Middle Ages, 117–19. *See also* Military theory
Warner, Marina, 10, 103
Wavrin, Jean de, 38
Wright, Nicholas, 90

Xaintrailles, Poton de, 70, 119

About the Author

STEPHEN W. RICHEY is a freelance researcher. Born and raised in Rochester, New York, he enlisted in the U.S. Army as a tank crewman in 1977. He graduated from the U.S. Military Academy at West Point in 1984 as a Second Lieutenant of tank troops. He has served out his military career in numerous places and in various capacities around the world, including Germany, the Persian Gulf War of 1991, humanitarian de-mining operations in Ethiopia, and earning his parachutist's wings at Fort Benning, Georgia. He presently serves as a part-time soldier in the office of Military Support to Civil Authorities of the Army National Guard in Washington State.